ELITE SERIES

EDITOR: MARTIN WINDROW

Inside the U.S. Army Today

Text by GORDON L. ROTTMAN

Colour plates by RON VOLSTAD

OSPREY PUBLISHING LONDON

Published in 1988 by
Osprey Publishing Ltd
Member company of the George Philip Group
12–14 Long Acre, London WC2E 9LP
© Copyright 1988 Osprey Publishing Ltd

British Library Cataloguing in Publication Data

Rottman, Gordon L.
    Inside the US army today.—(Osprey
    elite; V.20).
    1. United States. Army
    I. Title   II. Volstad, Ron
    355′.00973

    ISBN 0-85045-855-2

Filmset in Great Britain
Printed through Bookbuilders Ltd, Hong Kong

Artist's Note

Readers may care to note that the original paintings from which the colour plates in this book were prepared are available for private sale. All reproduction copyright whatsoever is retained by the publisher. All enquiries should be addressed to:

Ronald B. Volstad
P.O. Box 1577
Main Post Office
Edmonton
Alberta
Canada T5J 2N9

The publishers regret that they can enter into no correspondence upon this matter.

Acknowledgements

The author wishes to thank the Infantry School Public Affairs Office for providing many of the photographs. Additional photographic aid was provided by Paul Lemmer. Much of the unit background information was gleaned from the Association of the US Army's annual *Army Green Book*, *National Guard Almanac* and the American Society of Military Collectors' *Trading Post Magazine*. Unit organisation information was taken principally from various US Army Command and General Staff College publications. As always, I owe much to my wife, Enriqueta.

Abbreviations used:

Units:

Co	Company
Bty	Battery
Trp	Troop
Bn	Battalion
Sdn	Squadron
Bde	Brigade
Gp	Group
Regt	Regiment
Div	Division

Branches/Misc.:

Abn	Airborne
AC	Active Component
ADA	Air Defense Artillery
ACR	Armored Cavalry Regt.
Armd	Armored
ARNG	Army National Guard
Aslt	Assault
Avn	Aviation
Cav	Cavalry
FA	Field Artillery
Hel	Helicopter
Inf	Infantry
Lt	Light
Mech	Mechanized
MI	Military Intelligence
MP	Military Police
RC	Reserve Components
Sep	Separate
SF	Special Forces
SP	Self-Propelled
USAR	US Army Reserve

British readers should note that in order to avoid inconsistencies, American spelling is used throughout this text.

Inside the U.S. Army Today

Introduction

When originally conceived this book was to cover 'the US Army in the 1980s'. It soon became clear that this would have required two such books: for the Army of today is substantially different from that of even 1982, and it is still in the midst of change.

While the personality of the Army is unchanged, the organisation of its higher levels of command and combat formations, and the internal structure of its units have undergone major changes under the 'Army of Excellence' program. Originating in the early 1980s as the 'Division 86', and later 'Army 86' reorganisation programs, the 'AoE' goes far beyond 'just another reorganisation . . . change for change's sake'. The integration of high technology into new weapon, target acquisition, command, control, communications and intelligence (C³I), and logistical support systems has affected not only how units are organised, but how they interrelate with each other. By way of example, today's tank and mech. infantry battalions are so technology-oriented that it is no longer possible for a common organisation service support battalion to support a brigade. The new forward support battalions providing direct

A Drill Sergeant assists an initial entry soldier during M16A1 marksmanship training, an excellent program. (US Army—as are all other photographs not otherwise credited.)

support to brigades are internally structured depending on the specific mix and numbers of tank and mech. battalions, so heavy are their maintenance demands.

Unit organisation is also influenced by the Army's current doctrine, the AirLand Battle. It is argued by some that any 'new' tactic is not really new, but merely a slight variation on, if not virtually identical to, some older concept, but tagged with a catchy new name; they will follow this with a well-founded example, and a schematic of the concept will appear similar to the old tactic. What diagrams do not show is that under the influence of advanced weapons with more devastating effects, increased mobility, improved C^3I, high-speed communications, all-weather, day and night reconnaissance, surveillance and target acquisition, and sophisticated sustainment capabilities, the nature of the tactical concept changes drastically.

For a simple example, let us look at tank killing.

Initial entry soldiers negotiate the 'weaver' obstacle on the confidence course.

Certain Second World War German assault gun tactics appear similar to some of those used by the US Army today—on paper. But when comparing the capabilities of a 1944 assault gun mounting a 75mm kinetic energy gun with a range of about 1,000m, optical sights, and a maximum *road* speed of 20 mph, with those of an improved TOW anti-armor vehicle fitted with wire-guided missiles with a 3,000m range, thermal and light amplification poor visibility sighting systems, and a *cross-country* speed of 40 mph, a different picture emerges.

Higher command structures are also undergoing changes in an effort to enhance command and control, to pass intelligence information, to provide a more rapid response to quickly changing situations, and to make more effective use of manpower. This latter aspect has greatly influenced today's Army organisation due to the self-imposed ceiling of 780,000 active personnel; but even this is in danger of being reduced as Congress outlines a cut of 8,400 troops, which would reduce the Army's strength to its lowest in ten years. Manning limitations have caused the Army to reduce rifle

squads and self-propelled artillery crews from 11 to nine men. It also seeks weapons and other major equipment items which require less manpower to operate. Logistical units are being provided with improved material handling equipment in an effort to reduce their manning needs.

Even unit assignments and traditions have changed with the implementation of the Army Regimental System, an effort to achieve more unit cohesion and personnel stability—long a major, but often unaddressed aspect of the Army's manning.

The Troops

When conscription was eliminated in the early 1970s, the Army found itself with a very different kind of soldier. Initially the Volunteer Army (VOLAR) system had its faults; NCO corps dissatisfaction (due to lack of authority, a legacy from Vietnam), excessive drug abuse, racial problems, high indiscipline rates, and low education levels.

A number of factors have changed the face of today's Army. An aggressive NCO Development Program, with the motto 'Training is Sergeants' Business', demanding higher standards, is beginning to return the quality of NCOs to that of the mid-1960s. Education benefits, critical skill bonuses, improved family programs, and more challenging training goals have greatly increased troop morale, with the resultant spin-off of far fewer drug, discipline, and racial problems. More women are joining the Army and are incorporated into the ranks in the same way as their male counterparts; the Women's Army Corps (WAC) was disbanded in 1978. Though they are still restricted to non-combat rôles, many combat support skill fields are now open to the 83,000 women soldiers.

Today's high technology weapon and support systems demand better educated soldiers, and this has certainly been achieved. In 1980 only about half of the new recruits were high school graduates;

Pugil stick training is used to reinforce bayonet skills. These trainees are outfitted in protective helmets, torso shields, special gloves, and groin protectors.

92 per cent of today's recruits hold a diploma.

A soldier enlists for an eight-year service obligation (six years prior to 1986). Most will serve for three to four years on active duty, with the remainder either in the Individual Ready Reserve (subject to call-up in the event of war or a national emergency) or in an Army National Guard or Reserve troop unit, at individual choice.

The new soldier's first months are spent under the tutelage of the Training and Doctrine Command (TRADOC), where he will undertake eight weeks of Basic Training (BT) at one of nine Training Centers. Here the soldier will be introduced to Army life and discipline; will be taught how to drill, identify rank, live in the field, move and survive on the battlefield (especially in chemical and radiological environments); will learn basic first aid, qualify with the M16A1 rifle, and be shaped into fairly good physical condition. He is also taught to be more aggressive than his post-Vietnam counterparts, with the re-introduction of bayonet fighting and pugil stick training. These disciplines go beyond mere aggressive conditioning, being exten-

A Drill Sergeant demonstrates bayonet moves to a trainee. Both wear the Battle Dress Uniform (BDU).

sions of physical fitness, co-ordination, and agility. From there the soldier will go on to Advanced Individual Training (AIT), where he will be trained in one of the scores of Military Occupation Specialities (MOS). AIT may vary from six weeks to almost a year in length depending on the MOS; most are in the range of roughly two to three months. Combat arms branch MOSs (infantry, armor, field artillery, air defense artillery, and certain engineer MOSs) are conducted under One-Station Unit Training (OSUT). Here both BT and AIT are conducted in the same training unit with the same instructor cadre, thus providing continuity of training, e.g. infantry OSUT is conducted at Ft. Benning, Georgia and is 14 weeks long.

From there the soldier will be assigned to a troop unit which may be located in the US, Europe, the Pacific region, or elsewhere. Additional skill training may be provided through unit or post schools, special skill courses taught at specific training centers, or more advanced skills at branch schools as the soldier progresses through the ranks. Heavy emphasis is placed on realistic, 'hands-on', performance-oriented training.

These skills are driven by a task/conditions/standards training methodology, which

Infantry trainees firing the M249E1 squad automatic weapon (SAW). Hearing protection is highly emphasised by the Army: the trainees wear small, but effective ear plugs.

basically tells the soldier what the task is, the conditions under which it is to be accomplished, and the standards to be met in order to accomplish it. These are prescribed in Soldier's Manuals, one for each skill level (up to five) for every MOS. Skills common to all soldiers are tested annually, as are each soldier's specific MOS skills in the Skill Qualification Tests (SQT).

Unit training is made as realistic as resources and peacetime safety constraints permit. Particular importance is placed on weapons live firing—although with rising procurement costs, budget cuts, and high costs of advanced weapons munitions (a TOW missile costs over $2,000) much use is made of simulators and sub-caliber systems. Similar to individual skills, unit missions are also driven by task/conditions/standards and outlined in Army Training and Evaluation Programs (ARTEP), which prescribe specific actions to be conducted by a given type of unit's sub-units in order for the whole

to accomplish its missions. These are tied to the related individual skills.

Leadership

Long the backbone of the Army, the NCO corps has done much to 'self-police' itself and re-establish its authority and image. While it is possible for a first enlistment soldier to make the rank of sergeant, most are promoted after re-enlisting for a second tour. However, NCO preparation begins while the soldier is a Specialist 4, when he may attend the Primary Leadership Development Course. As he progresses up through the NCO grades, additional courses are taken at each skill level to include Basic, Primary, and Advanced NCO Courses, in addition to advanced MOS and special skill courses. NCO promotion is based not only on time in grade and service, but on demonstrated skill and on meeting the NCO education requirements.

Officers are obtained from a number of sources. A large percentage are commissioned through the Senior Reserve Officer Training Corps (SROTC)[1] conducted at colleges and universities. A civilian

As an instructor looks on, an infantry trainee fires a 40mm M203 grenade launcher mounted on an M16A1 rifle. Though seemingly awkward to fire, it is an extremely accurate weapon out to 350 metres.

[1]Junior ROTC is conducted in high schools as a military orientation course and does not lead to commissioning.

aspiring to become an officer will attend four years of ROTC while obtaining a college degree, his last two years while under contract to the Army, from which he receives monetary aid. Upon graduation he is commissioned as a second lieutenant and is obligated to the Army for eight years, usually four to six years on active duty. Other officers are trained through branch Officer Candidate Schools (OCS). A small percentage are graduates of the US Military Academy at West Point, N.Y. A very small percentage are obtained through direct commissioning, usually individuals possessing special technical skills. Physicians, nurses, and chaplains are obtained through special programs.

Regardless of the source of commission, the new officer will attend his Basic Branch Course while still a second lieutenant. While a captain he will attend his Advanced Branch Course, and most majors and lieutenant colonels will attend the Command and General Staff College at Ft. Levenworth, Kansas. Higher level courses, both Army and joint service, also exist. Civilian education is far from neglected as all officers are required to possess a college degree. Much emphasis is placed on obtaining still higher levels of education, with Ph.Ds and doctorates not uncommon among senior officers (much to the confusion of many congressmen dictating defense cuts, who have found themselves dealing with officers with a higher education than themselves). This writer can assure the reader that the Army's officers are a far cry from the narrow-minded, overly-militant stereotypes depicted by Hollywood and envisioned by the media.

Warrant officers are a category of officers possessing technical skills. They receive a warrant rather than a commission and do not have command authority, but supervisory authority. They do have most of the same privileges as commissioned officers. Warrant officers are often former NCOs who have been warranted due to their abilities in special skill fields. They will also attend the Warrant Officer Course (WOC), and often more advanced technical courses. Examples of warrant officer duties include various automotive and electronic maintenance tasks, and those of medical technicians, intelligence specialists, and helicopter pilots (commissioned officers are also pilots).

An infantry trainee, on a hot day, prepares to fire an M72A3 light anti-tank weapon (LAW). Though not obvious, a 35mm sub-caliber device is fitted inside the launch tube.

Weapon Systems

While space only permits a cursory look at the Army's major weapon systems, an overview is necessary to fully demonstrate not only how the impact of technological advances has improved the capability of the Army to fight, but to show how it has affected organisation and tactics. Technology has changed the modern battlefield by the increase in weapons lethality, mobility, surveillance and target acquisition, C^3I, and sustainment.

A wide variety of new weapon systems began to be fielded in the early 1980s; many existing systems were also greatly improved. Many of these systems offer more than just a quantitative improvement over the system they replace. Often they are advanced to the point that a one-on-one replacement is unnecessary; e.g. a Cobra-equipped attack helicopter battalion has 21 × AH-1S Cobras, while an Apache attack battalion has 18 × AH-64s (both have 13 × OH-58C scouts).

To more readily implement the fielding of new weapon systems they are issued in Unit Sets accompanied by maintenance and compatible

A Drill Sergeant instructs infantry trainees in land navigation. The corporal's stripes on a black armband indentify an acting squad leader.

service support equipment, since their sophistication often requires special support requirements, e.g. a tank battalion undergoing modernisation is issued 58 × M1A1 tanks, but also receives in the same time period: 5-ton ammunition trucks, 1½-ton ammunition trailers, 30 training days of 120mm ammunition, initial M1A1 repair part stocks, M1A1 maintenance and test sets, Maintenance Equipment and New Equipment Training Teams from the Armor School to train unit personnel, and even newly assigned school-trained maintenance personnel. These resources ensure that the unit is ready to fight, and is not devalued by shortages of critical items.

M1 Abrams Main Battle Tank Replacing earlier model tanks at a rapid pace, the M1 is an extremely advanced design. Its agility, special armor, and sophisticated targeting systems make it the primary ground combat weapon system. It is armed with a 105mm gun, 1 × .50 cal. and 2 × 7.62mm machineguns (MG). The improved IPM1 offers enhanced survivability and suspension systems. The M1A1 has a 120mm gun and adds a nuclear, biological, chemical (NBC) protection system. Fielding of the M1 began in 1981, the IPM1 in 1984, and the M1A1 in 1985. Current plans call for the production of 2,374 M1s, 894 IPM1s, and 4,576 M1A1s, the final 2,499 of which will have the new depleted uranium, steel enveloped armor. M1s and IPM1s already issued to units in Europe are being returned for reissue to stateside units when the former receive M1A1s[1].

M60A3TTS Main Battle Tank Still the mainstay of most RC and a few AC tank units, the M60 was adopted in the early 1960s. All models have been upgraded to the M60A3TTS (tank thermal system) with further improvements scheduled, including appliqué armor. It is armed with a 105mm gun and one each .50 cal. and 7.62mm MGs.

M48A5 Patton Main Battle Tank The M48A5 has been extensively upgraded over earlier models to almost M60A3 standards, to include the fitting of a

[1]See Vanguard 41, *The M1 Abrams Battle Tank*

105mm gun. It also mounts a .50 cal. and 2 × 7.62mm MGs. Some RC tank units are still equipped with it[2].

All of the above tanks have a four-man crew.

M2 Bradley Infantry Fighting Vehicle The M2 IFV is an actual combat vehicle from which infantrymen can fight and not a 'battlefield taxi' which merely transports them, as did earlier armored personnel carriers. The amphibious M2 was designed to keep pace with the M1 tank and to possess its own substantial tank-killing capability. Armed with a 25mm 'chain gun', 7.62mm MG, 6 × 5.56mm firing-port weapons, and a twin-tubed TOW missile launcher, it carries a nine-man rifle squad, three of whom are required to crew it. Fielding of the M2 began in 1983 and of the upgraded M2A1 in 1986. A total of 6,882 IFVs are scheduled for production.[3]

M3 Bradley Cavalry Fighting Vehicle The armored cavalry version of the M2 IFV, the M3 CFV is very similar, but carries only a five-man cavalry or scout squad, three being crewmen. It has the same armament as the M2, but lacks the firing port weapons. It is issued to armored cavalry troops and scout platoons of mech. infantry and tank battalions. About 3,300 will be produced.[3]

M113 series Armored Personnel Carriers A large number of variants of this ubiquitous and versatile vehicle have been developed since its introduction in 1959, and it will still be in use well past the year 2000. The M113A2 and A3 versions are still the standard APC in most RC and some AC mech. infantry units. It carries an 11-man rifle squad, two of whom crew it. In armored cavalry troops and mech. infantry and tank battalion scout platoons it is crewed by three to four men. The M113 is armed with only a .50 cal. MG. Over 26,000 M113s and variants are in use[4].

M113 Variants A large number of M113 variant vehicles have been developed for special purposes so as to provide protection from artillery and small arms fire, and to permit the weapon or support systems they mount to keep pace with APCs and tanks:

M106A2 107mm (4.2-in.) M30 mortar carrier
M125A2 81mm M29A1 or M252 mortar carrier
M548 6-ton cargo carrier (unarmored)

M577A2 command post vehicle
M688 Lance missile loader and transporter
M727 Improved HAWK AD missile carrier
M730 Chaparral AD missile carrier
M741 Vulcan 20mm M163 AD gun carrier
M752 Lance missile launch vehicle
M981 artillery fire support team (FIST) vehicle
M1015 electronic warfare shelter carrier
M1059 smoke generator carrier

M901 Improved TOW Vehicle The ITV, although an M113 variant, is discussed separately due to its importance to mech. infantry units. It mounts a twin TOW launcher in an elevating turret permitting the vehicle to remain concealed during firing. It also has a 7.62mm MG and several advanced day and night sights greatly enhancing its effectiveness. The ITV has a four-man crew, which can dismount and set up a ground TOW launcher.

TOW Missile System The TOW (Tube-launched, Optically tracked Wire command-link missile) is the Army's principal heavy anti-armor system. It is found mounted on Bradley fighting vehicles, various wheeled tactical vehicles, the ITV, and Cobra attack helicopters as well as the M220A1 ground mount. The improved TOW 2 was first fielded in 1983, with still further modifications scheduled to both launchers and missiles. Its current range is 3,000m (3,750m from helicopters).

M101A1 105mm Towed Howitzer Adopted in 1939 as

Second lieutenants attending the Infantry Officers' Basic Course maneuver during a live fire exercise at Ft. Benning, Ga.

See Vanguard 29, *The M47 and M48 Patton Tanks*
See Vanguard 43, *The M2 Bradley Infantry Fighting Vehicle*
See Vanguard 34, *M113 Series*

the M2, the M101A1 is still in use by many RC units, although it is being replaced by M102s transferred from AC units. It has an 11,270m range (14,500 with rocket-assisted projectiles—RAP). All 105mm howitzers have a seven-man crew.

M102 105mm Towed Howitzer Fielded in 1966, this lightweight 105mm is being replaced in AC units by the M119. Its range is 11,500m (15,000 with RAP).

M119 105mm Towed Howitzer Currently in the process of replacing the M102 in AC units, it will later be issued to RC units as well. First issued in 1988, it is the US-produced version of the British-designed L119 Light Gun. Its range is 14,300m (19,500m with RAP).

M114A1 155mm Towed Howitzer Adopted in 1942 as the M1, the M114A1 is still in use by most RC medium FA battalions, but scheduled for replacement by the M198. Its range is 20,100m. All 155mm towed howitzers are manned by a crew of 11.

M198 155mm Towed Howitzer Fielding began in 1976 of the M114A1's replacement. It is in use by all AC medium FA units, and a few RC units have also received it. Its range is 22,000m (30,000m with RAP).

M109A2/A3 155mm SP Howitzer In use since 1963, the M109 series is a fully-tracked, fully armored SP howitzer crewed by six men. Its range is 18,100m (24,000m with RAP). The system is currently being upgraded under the Howitzer Improvement Program, which will, among other improvements, give it the same range as the M198. The M108 105mm SP howitzer was phased out by the early 1970s and replaced by the 155mm.

All 155mm howitzers can fire the Copperhead, a laser-guided projectile which can hit a moving tank at up to 16km.

M110A2 203mm SP Howitzer The '8-inch' is mounted on a fully-tracked, but open chassis. Manned by 13 men, its range is 23,000m (29,000m with RAP). Some RC units are still equipped with the shorter barrelled M110 with somewhat less range. The M107 175mm SP gun was phased out of US service in the 1970s and replaced by the 203mm.

Artillery ammunition is available in several different types depending on caliber. Besides high

A student sniper zeros in on a target with an M21 sniper rifle while attending a three-week sniper course. Note the 'ghillie' camouflage suit.

explosive, white phosphorus, and screening smoke, several highly advanced 155mm munitions (all containing numerous submunitions) have been developed to include: dual purpose improved conventional munitions (light anti-armor and anti-personnel), remote anti-armor mines, and area denial munitions. The 155mm and 203mm howitzers are also nuclear capable.

M270 Multiple-Launch Rocket System The 12-round free-flight MLRS is mounted on a derivative of the Bradley chassis. Manned by a crew of three, its range is over 30,000m. The rocket itself is 13ft long and 9 in. in diameter. The M77 dual purpose improved conventional munition warhead has 644 submunitions, making it a devastating area fire weapon.

Lance Battlefield Support Missile First deployed in 1972, the Lance is transported by a fully-tracked carrier. It can be tipped with a nuclear or conventional submunitions warhead and has a range of over 75km. Eight battalions are in service.

M168 20mm Vulcan AD Gun This radar-controlled six-barrel gun is found mounted on the M741 carrier as the M163 AD gun system. The M167

two-wheeled towed version is also used. Its range against aircraft is 1,200m and 2,200m against ground targets; rate of fire is selectable to either 1,000 or 3,000 rpm.

Chaparral AD Missile System Mounting four modified Sidewinder missiles, the Chaparral is transported on an M730 fully-tracked carrier, although a towed version is available. The missile is infrared-seeking and has a range of over 5km.

Improved HAWK AD Missile System Both SP and towed IHAWK launchers are in use, each mounting three of the radar-guided missiles. Entering service in 1960, the improved IHAWK was fielded in 1972. Its range is over 40km.

Patriot AD Missile System Deployment of the first of these highly advanced systems began in 1985, with six battalions now fielded and four more to come on line in the next two years. The towed launcher mounts four missiles. Its range is classified, but is most impressive.

AH-1S Cobra Attack Helicopter Developed in 1965 as the Army's first dedicated gunship, the Cobra has been modified over the years into the AH-1S, designed to better fight and survive on the modern battlefield. Crewed by two men, it mounts a three-barrel 20mm cannon, 38 × 2.75 in. Hydra 70 rockets (5,200m range), and 8 × TOW 2 missiles (3,750m range). Cruise speed is 120 knots (221km per hour). Over 700 Cobras are in use[1].

AH-64 Apache Attack Helicopter The advanced AH-64 was first deployed in 1986. It mounts a 30mm 'chain gun' and either 16 × Hellfire missiles, or 8 × Hellfires and 38 × 2.75 in. rockets, or 76 × 2.75 in. rockets. The Hellfire is a laser homing anti-armor missile with a range of over 6,000m. The Apache's cruise speed is 175 knots (320km per hour). A total of 593 AH-64s will be procured to equip 29 battalions[1].

Laser-guided munitions such as the artillery-fired Copperhead and the Hellfire are guided to the target by illuminating it with a laser spot generated from a laser designator mounted in another AH-64, an OH-58C scout helicopter, a FIST vehicle, or a ground-mounted/hand-held model used by dismounted personnel. This means that the Copperhead may be fired from a great distance, or the Hellfire launched, with the AH-64 departing, while the target is illuminated from another location. This assures an almost first round hit probability.

[1]See Vanguard 44, *Anti-Tank Helicopters*

A rifleman and grenadier armed with improved M16A2 rifles engage targets from a fighting position. (Colt Firearms)

Reserve Components

Long the butt of jokes and outright derision, the 'weekend warriors' of the Army National Guard (ARNG) and US Army Reserve (USAR) have changed their image and rôle drastically in recent years. With the institution of VOLAR and the decision to maintain the Active Army at 780,000 troops, the Army was forced to seek manpower-saving initiatives and efficiency enhancements. The capability of the Army to respond to a wide diversity of worldwide contingencies also forced planners to look outside the active forces for their manpower and equipment needs.

The importance of the Reserve Components (RC) in past wars has often been under-emphasised. In the First World War a total of 17 ARNG and 18 Army of the United States (AUS—made up of Reservists and transferred to the USAR after the war) divisions were deployed to Europe along with the eight Regular Army (RA) divisions. A similar situation existed in the Second World War with 19 ARNG, 29 USAR/AUS, and 39 RA[2] divisions serving. Of the eight divisions which served in Korea, two were ARNG. A number of battalion and smaller RC units served in Vietnam.

In the past though, the ARNG and USAR had the luxury of time—time to train after mobilisation and prior to actual deployment, and time to receive new equipment rolling off the assembly lines. The speed at which situations develop and escalate today, and the expected intensity of future conflicts have eliminated this luxury. Today's RC units train with the philosophy of the 'come-as-you-are war' i.e. the equipment you train with and the personnel on-hand is what a unit will deploy with when mobilised.

ARNG personnel are recruited by state recruiters operating out of area armories, while USAR personnel are recruited by Reserve recruiters working in Active Army recruiting stations. Both categories of personnel enlist for eight years, usually with four or six years spent in a troop unit and the balance in the Individual Ready Reserve. Once enlisted they undertake Basic Training and AIT alongside AC personnel for up to six months before

[2]The drastic increase of RA divisions was principally due to the activation of 16 armored and five airborne divisions.

returning to their RC unit. AC personnel may also join the Guard or Reserve directly from active duty. Officers are procured through ROTC commissions, active OCSs, state OCSs (ARNG only), or directly from active duty.

Since RC personnel are 'part-timers', someone has to keep the organisation running between drills. This is accomplished by Active Guard/Reserve (AGR) program personnel assigned to units on a full-time basis. These officers and NCOs perform day-to-day operations/training, administrative, supply, and maintenance functions. They are further supplemented by military technicians and civilian employees, who are Reservists themselves.

A vast number of resources have been made available to RC units to increase their readiness: issue of modern equipment, the same enlisted and officer individual skill requirements as their AC counterparts, additional training areas, more access to AC schools and courses, more RC schools and courses, increased unit and individual training opportunities with AC units, and a vast increase in participation in overseas deployment exercises.

3rd Bn., 75th Ranger Regt. troops exit a C-141 with T-10M parachutes. Though considered outmoded by some, the Army still places a great deal of reliance on the capabilities of parachute-delivered troops.

A 197th Inf. Bde. trooper mans an M2 .50 cal. machine gun (fitted with a blank firing device) atop a 2½ ton cargo truck's ring mount. This provides a good view of the plastic camouflage net.

Several programs affiliate RC units with AC forces proving beneficial to both. One of the most effective programs is CAPSTONE: RC units are assigned to specific AC units to provide needed units not in their structure. Other programs align larger RC formations with similar AC counterparts for training support. These affiliation programs go beyond joint training, and allow RC units to become familiar with their active units' leaders and staffs, standard operating procedures, wartime contingency plans, and overseas areas of operation. These units are also usually equipped with the same weapon systems, vehicles, and other major equipment items, especially communications gear, as their AC parent formation.

Possibly the single most beneficial aspect of these programs is the opportunity for RC units and individuals to deploy and train overseas. Certain segments of the media are often quick to condemn overseas training for RC units as costly, dangerous,

An M113A3 armored personnel carrier at Ft. Erwin, Calif., the National Training Center. The M113 is still the mainstay of many mechanized infantry units.

and of little benefit ('a unit can train just as well locally as overseas'). Any real soldier knows that tactical training is only a small part of combat readiness; logistics is the key to success, and deploying overseas is perhaps one of the most difficult of logistical and co-ordinative tasks encountered. Quite simply, the only effective way to train for it is to do it.

RC units generally train one weekend a month. A weekend drill—or officially, a multiple unit training assembly, (MUTA)—may consist of individual or unit training plus maintenance and administrative functions. Some units, such as aviation and airborne, may have additional drill periods conducted on Friday nights, other weekends, or even weekdays. Individuals may be given additional training assemblies (ATA) to perform training on weekdays. Active duty training (ADT) is performed when Guardsmen and Reservists attend training courses and exercises with active schools and units. Annual training (AT), referred to as 'summer camp', is 15 days in duration and usually conducted at active posts. Many units have begun to conduct some of their ATs in the winter so as to prepare them better for European deployment. Increased emphasis is also being placed on overseas deployment training (ODT) with many RC units conducting their AT in Europe, Korea, Egypt, and Central or South America. ODT AT is three weeks in length.

Virtually every AC formation relies on RC units to some degree. Almost 50 per cent of the total Army combat forces are provided by the RC as the Army attempts to achieve the 'Total Force Policy' or 'One Army' concept. To an outsider the existence of two parallel reserve forces may seem redundant; the rôles and structure of the two RC organisations are different with each having its own purposes, but both are aimed towards a common goal.

Army National Guard

This oldest of the RC organisations has its origins in the original colonial and later state militias. Guardsmen take a dual oath of allegiance, to the President of the United States and their state governor. Each of the 50 states, District of Columbia, Puerto Rico, Virgin Islands, and Guam have their own Guard, termed e.g., the Iowa Army

National Guard. Each state's ARNG is under the control of the governor through the adjutant general. The AG is an appointed officer, usually with the rank of major-general, who oversees the state Adjutant-General Department (Dept. of Military Affairs in some cases).

The Guard may be called up by the governor to assist with natural disasters, civil disturbances, and other state emergencies, and paid with state funds. Though under state control and administered by the state, the Guard's funding and equipment are furnished by the Federal government through each state's US Property and Fiscal Office. The state provides the land for unit armories, but the Federal government funds their construction. The Guard may be federalised by the President for the same reasons the state governors can call them up, as well as for national emergencies. The President can mobilise as many as 200,000 ARNG (and USAR) personnel without a declaration of war or national emergency. These 54 sometimes seemingly 'private armies' are jointly administered by the National Guard Bureau in Washington, itself directly subordinate to the Department of the Army.

The ARNG currently consists of over 440,000 troops organised into 3,600 units in 2,600 communities: 12 combat divisions; 22 separate combat brigades & regiments; 37 combat support

Though not normally issued, the M113A3 APC can be fitted with bolt-on space laminated armor and a .50 cal. M2 machine gun shield.

A 197th Inf. Bde. rifle squad dismounts from an M113A3 APC through the rear troop door.

An M60A3TTS main battle tank at the National Training Center. The tubes above the 105mm gun are main gun firing simulators. A D7 dozer is in the background.

& service support brigades; over 300 separate battalion-sized units; over 700 separate companies & detachments.

ARNG units are predominantly combat and combat support, with a substantial share of service support units. The units assigned to a given state vary greatly, based principally on population density, but in recent years the location of their AC CAPSTONE or ROUNDOUT formations have been taken into consideration more often. A given Guard formation can have some of its units in other states, but even though subordinate to it, they are still under the direct control of their state's AG Department.

US Army Reserve

The USAR is directly under Federal control, being administered by the Department of the Army's Office of the Chief, Army Reserve. What is referred to as the Ready Reserve is made up of two organisations, the Selected Reserve and the Individual Ready Reserve (IRR).

The Selected Reserve has about 310,000 personnel organised into troop units. USAR units are not affiliated with states but are controlled by 21 Army Reserve Commands (ARCOM), themselves supervised by numbered armies; a given ARCOM commands units in several adjacent states. (One, however, the 7th ARCOM, administers USAR units and individuals in Europe.) While the USAR does possess some combat units (three each infantry and FA brigades), most are training, combat support, and combat service support units located in over 1,100 Reserve Centers:
12 major commands (excluding ARCOMs, MACs, MTCs); 12 training divisions; 16 combat support & service support brigades; over 60 separate battalions; over 100 army hospitals; over 3,200 separate companies & detachments.

Training is a key function of the Reserves. USAR schools are located across the country, offering individual skill MOS training and NCO courses to all USAR and ARNG personnel. The two maneuver area commands (MAC) possess planning staffs which conduct command post and field training exercises for ARNG and USAR groups, brigades, and divisions. The nine maneuver training commands (MTC) offer similar support to battalions.

The training divisions consist of staffs, support personnel, and drill instructors as the cadre for training brigades and battalions. In the event of mobilisation these units would deploy to an assigned post, establish a Basic Training and AIT center, and begin producing combat trained troops from conscripts/volunteers, e.g. the 95th Div. (Training) in Midwest City, Oklahoma would set up housekeeping at Ft. Chaffee, Arkansas. Most of these divisions are structured to train infantrymen and various high density, moderate skill combat support MOS soldiers, i.e. mechanics, truck drivers, radio operators, wiremen, personnel and supply specialists and cooks. Some are more specialised such as the 85th Div., which would train tankers and armored cavalrymen. A similar unit, the 402nd FA Bde. (Training) of Lawton, Oklahoma, would move to Ft. Sill, Oklahoma and train artillerymen.

The IRR is an organisation of over 300,000 Reservists in various categories. This includes individual Reservists who have undertaken basic and MOS training, but are not assigned to an RC troop unit; Individual Mobilization Augmentees who are pre-identified to fill AC unit wartime duty positions; individuals who attend drills in an unpaid status since duty positions are not locally available

A ground-mounted M220A1 TOW missile system is prepared for firing. Mounted above its main tracker (sight) is an AN/TAS-4A thermal-imaging night sight.

(they do receive retirement credit); and individuals separated from active duty and Guardsmen and Reservists released from troop units who have not completed their eight-year obligation. The IRR are administered by the Army Reserve Personnel Center in St. Louis, Missouri. These individuals may be recalled to active duty in the event of war or national emergency, or they may later join a ARNG or USAR unit.

An M1 Abrams main battle tank moves down a range road. Its low profile can be appreciated when compared against the height of the tank commander.

Organisation

The organisation of a given type of troop unit is governed by its Table of Organisation and Equipment (TOE). This outlines the authorised strength levels by rank and MOS, internal subunit structure, and distribution of weapons, vehicles and equipment. However, few units are actually organised according to the base TOE because of its assigned mission, area of operations, and availability of unit equipment and weapon systems (major end items), or it may provide for substitutes for major end items. The actual organisation of a specific unit is specified by its Modified TOE. The MTOE permits a unit to be tailored to meet its specific mission requirements. It may also be structured to place a unit at reduced manning and equipment levels. One-of-a-kind organisations and agencies are governed by Tables of Distribution and Allowance (TDA), which permit their structure to be developed as their rôle requires.

There are three principal TOE series. The H-series was developed in the early 1970s, and continually updated to keep pace with new equipment developments, manning requirements, and tactics. Armor and mech. infantry units with older model tanks and APCs are included under the H-series as are standard infantry, as opposed to light infantry. The J-series was introduced in the mid-1980s to meet the requirements of the Army of Excellence reorganisation. Armor and mech. infantry units equipped with M1 tanks and Bradley fighting vehicles come under this series. The light, airborne, and air assault infantry units come under the L-series.

Formations larger than divisions have no fixed organisation, but have units assigned or attached as their mission requires, permitting organisational flexibility and restructuring as mission requirements change.

Corps organisation varies, having evolved into the Army's principal combat, combat support, and combat service support formation. Some corps units are provided by the RC. Contingency corps (XVIII Abn. and I Corps) are organised for low

Front view of an M2 Bradley infantry fighting vehicle. Both the 25mm M242 Bushmaster 'chain gun' and co-axial 7.62mm M240 machine gun can be seen. Above the driver's hatch are smoke grenade dischargers.

and mid-intensity conflict deployment and consist principally of light forces. Heavy corps (III, V and VII Corps) are structured to face European threat mechanised forces. A representative heavy corps established for a theater of operations may include:

HQ and HQ Company, Corps
2–5 Divisions (types vary)
1–3 Separate Brigades (types vary)
Armored Cavalry Regiment
HQ & HQ Battery, Corps Artillery
2–4 FA Brigades
FA Target Acquisition Battalion
ADA Brigade
Engineer Brigade
MP Brigade
MI Brigade (Combat Electronic Warfare
    Intelligence)
Aviation or Cavalry Air Combat Brigade
Signal Brigade
Chemical Brigade or Group
Anti-armor Battalion
Psychological Operations Battalion

The Corps Support Command (COSCOM) consists of transport, supply, POL (petroleum, oil, lubricants), ammunition, maintenance, medical, and support units of brigade, group, and battalion size as required to support the corps' mission.

Divisions, categorised as either heavy or light, are the largest tactical formation with a fixed TOE and as such are the principal maneuver forces. Heavy divisions include armored, mech. infantry, and H-series infantry. Light divisions are the light infantry, airborne, air assault, and motorised formations.

For all practical purposes, the armored and mech. infantry divisions are identical, except for the mix of maneuver battalions; but any given division's actual organisation will vary. A mech. division's 'standard' strength is 16,600 troops while that of an armored division is 16,300. The 'division base' consists of combat support units that directly support the division and its subordinate combat units:

HQ & HQ Company, Division
ADA Battalion
Engineer Combat Battalion
MI Battalion (CEWI)

A rifle squad dismounts from an M2 Bradley IFV, providing excellent side and rear views. The box on the turret side houses the twin-tube TOW launcher, here folded down to the non-fire mode. The infantryman on the ramp carries an M47 Dragon missile system.

The HMMWV (high mobility, multipurpose wheeled vehicle), or 'Hum-Vee', is one of the principal vehicles used by the 9th Inf.Div.(Motorized), but is also replacing the $\frac{1}{4}$ ton 'jeep' utility vehicle in most other combat units. Available in a number of versions, this model mounts an M220A1 TOW missile system.

Signal Battalion
MP Company
Chemical Company

The Division Artillery (DIVARTY) contains all field artillery assets: HQ & HQ Battery (HHB), three FA Battalions, MLRS Battery, and Target Acquisition Battery. The Aviation Brigade, often called a Cavalry Brigade, was added in 1985–87 and consists of: HQ & HQ Company (HHC), Armored Cavalry Squadron, Attack Helicopter Battalions (two in Germany, one in the US), Assault Helicopter Company, and Command Aviation Company. The Division Support Command (DISCOM) consists of three Forward Support Battalions (one per brigade) containing an HQ & HQ Detachment (HHD) and Supply, Maintenance, and Medical Companies. The Main Support Battalion has an HHD and Supply and Service, Transport, Light Maintenance, Heavy Maintenance, Missile Support, and Medical Support Companies. The DISCOM also has an Aircraft Maintenance Company to support the aviation brigade.

Standard division structure calls for three Maneuver Brigades; some Active divisions have only two, but an ARNG 'roundout' separate brigade is aligned with these. Two-brigade divisions also lack one each FA and forward support battalions, engineer company, and armored cavalry troop, these units being supplied by its roundout brigade. Up to two additional separate brigades may be attached to a division in combat. A brigade can control up to five maneuver battalions, but three to four is the norm. A three-brigade division will normally have nine or ten maneuver battalions assigned, which may be attached to any given brigade as the tactical situation demands.

A three-brigade armored division usually has six tank and four mech. infantry battalions, while its mechanised counterpart will have five of each if in Germany, but only four mech. if in the US. In combat a brigade will deploy with its maneuver battalions and a number of divisional units placed in direct support: FA and forward support battalions, engineer company, and various teams and platoons from other divisional units.

Heavy maneuver battalions are the principal fire and maneuver units; their organisation varies depending on the TOE: *H-series Mech. Infantry*— HHC, three Rifle Companies (14 × M113-series APCs), Combat Support Company (CSC). *J-series Mech. Infantry*—HHC, four Rifle Companies (13 × M2 IFVs); Anti-armor Company (12 × M901 ITVs). *H-series Infantry*—HHC, three Rifle Companies, CSC. *H-series Tank*—HHC, three Tank Companies (17 × M60A3 or M48A5 tanks), CSC. *J-series Tank*—HHC, four Tank Companies (14 × M1 tanks).

HHCs consist of the battalion staff, headquarters sections; communications, maintenance, support (supply and mess), and medical platoons. J-series battalions include the scout and mortar platoons in the HHC since they have no CSC. H-series CSCs have scout, mortar, and anti-armor (TOW) platoons. Rifle and Tank Companies have an HQ and three platoons. Rifle platoons have an HQ (one M2 or M113 if mech.) and three rifle squads (each with an M2 or M113 if mech.). Each rifle squad has an M47 Dragon wire-guided anti-tank/assault missile system. H-series tank platoons have five tanks while J-series have four; with two tanks in the company HQ.

H-series Rifle Companies have a mortar platoon with 3 × 81mm M29A1s; mounted in M125 carriers in mech. units, J-series Rifle Companies have no mortars due to the increase in divisional artillery. H-series CSC mortar platoons have 4 × 107mm M30s; mounted in M106 carriers if mechanised J-series battalion mortar platoons field either 6 × 81mm M252 or 107mm M30 mortars mounted in M125 or M106 carriers.

In combat heavy maneuver battalions are organised into Task Forces, achieved by cross-attaching companies between battalions. It is seldom that battalions will fight 'pure', i.e. without cross-attachment. A mech. infantry battalion may have one of its rifle companies detached and attached to a tank battalion, in exchange for a tank company. However, it is possible for a given battalion to retain all of its companies and still receive an additional one through cross-attachment. A 'company slice' of HHC service support elements accompanies a company for this attachment. Other small brigade and divisional elements may also be attached, e.g. an engineer platoon, Stinger teams (one per company), ground surveillance radar teams, etc.

Likewise there will be cross-attachment between companies thus forming Company Teams, e.g. a tank company may have a rifle platoon attached and may or may not lose a tank platoon. Anti-armor sections are attached from the anti-armor company or CSC, FIST or fire support teams (artillery/mortar forward observers) are attached from a supporting FA battalion.

The H-series ARNG infantry divisions are similarly organised; however, they have no air

An AN/PRD-10 radio direction-finding system is but one of many examples of how high technology equipment can be made man-portable.

Infantrymen attending the Light Leader Course—an especially rigorous course for light infantry NCOs and junior officers—rappel from a UH-6oA Blackhawk helicopter.

defense or MI battalions[1], and aviation brigades are not yet fully formed. DIVARTY has three battalions of towed 105mm howitzers and one of mixed 155mm towed and 203mm SP. It is proposed to change this to one SP and two towed 155mm howitzer battalions and add an MLRS battery. H-series armored and mech. infantry DIVARTYs have one 203mm and three 155mm SP battalions. The DISCOM is not organised into forward support battalions supporting given brigades, but rather into common branch battalions: Supply and Transport, Maintenance, and Medical, plus Adjutant General and Finance Companies (both corps units under the J-series). Forward Area Support Teams (FASTs) are formed from the battalions' elements to support each brigade. Eight infantry

and one each mech. infantry and tank battalions are normally assigned.

FA Battalion organisation also varies depending on TOE series; each has an HHB and three firing batteries. J-series 155mm M198 towed and M109 SP howitzer batteries have eight tubes. H-series 105mm M101A1/M102 and 155mm M114A1 towed and M109 SP batteries have six tubes. H-series 155mm/203mm battalions have two batteries with six 155mm M114A1 towed and one with four 203mm M110 SP. H-series pure 203mm M110 SP batteries have four tubes while J-series have eight. H-series battalions also have a Service Battery, eliminated in the J-series, except in 203mm battalions. MLRS batteries have 9 × M270 MLRSs. Lance missile batteries have two launcher systems. The 203mm, MLRS, and Lance battalions are corps artillery units, to which towed and SP 155mm battalions are also assigned; three to five mixed types of FA battalions to an FA brigade.

The ADA Battalion has an HHB and three Gun/Stinger Batteries, each with 12 × 20mm M163 Vulcan SP guns and 15 Stinger missile teams,

<hr>

[1]Separate Chaparral ADA Battalions, assigned to the ARNG's 111th ADA Bde., are aligned with most ARNG divisions. USAR MI Battalions are also aligned with each ARNG division since Federal law prohibits MI units being under State control.

the latter for attachment to tank and infantry companies and FA batteries. Chaparral, Patriot, and Improved HAWK AD missile battalions, as well as Gun/Stinger Battalions, are assigned to corps' and echelon above corps' ADA brigades.

Armored cavalry units carry the traditional cavalry titles of squadron (battalion-sized) and troop (company-sized)[2]. They too are organised under different TOEs: J-series heavy division squadrons have an HQ & HQ Troop (HHT) and two each Armored Cavalry and Air Cavalry Troops, H-series divisional squadrons have an HHT, an Air Cavalry and three Armored Cavalry Troops. J-series troops have 12 × M3 CFVs, 9 × M1 tanks, and 2 × M106 SP 107mm mortars. H-series troops substitute M113 APCs for the M3s and M48A5 or M60A3 tanks for the M1s.

Armored Cavalry Regiments (ACR) are brigade-sized forces tasked principally with fighting

Further capabilities of the UH-60A are demonstrated as it sling-loads an HMMWV.

the corps covering force battle, i.e. to engage and wear down enemy forces before they reach the main battle zone. They also perform reconnaissance in force, screening, flank security, and deep attack missions; divisional squadrons conduct similar missions. The ACR has three squadrons organised differently from divisions: HHT, three Armored Cavalry Troops, a Tank Company, and a 155mm SP Howitzer Battery. The Service Support Squadron is similar to a separate infantry brigade's battalion. They may or may not have a Combat Aviation Squadron, ADA Battery, and MI, Engineer, and Chemical Companies.

Separate maneuver brigades may be Infantry (three inf. battalions), Mech. Infantry (one tank and two mech. battalions), or Armored (one mech. and two tank battalions), but can control up to five battalions. Mech. and armored brigades have an SP 155mm FA battalion while infantry brigades have a 105mm towed battalion. All have a Service

---

[2]AC Long Range Surveillance Detachments (LRSD) were organic to divisional armored cavalry squadrons until 1987 when they were reassigned to the M1 battalions. ARNG LRSDs remain in the cavalry squadrons since they have no M1 battalions. See Elite 13, *US Army Rangers and LRRP Units 1942–87.*

An AH-1S Cobra attack helicopter armed with eight TOW missiles and a 20mm gun.

Support Battalion with one each Supply and Transport, Maintenance, and Medical Companies. The H-series infantry brigade also has an Administrative Company. There is also an Armored Cavalry Troop, Engineer Combat Company, and in a few, an MI Company.

The Light Infantry Divisions, first formed in 1984–85, are intended for deployment to possible low-intensity conflict regions. Their organisation, equipment allocation, and manning are guided by the principle that they must be capable of airlift by no more than 500 C-141 aircraft sorties. With a strength of only 10,770, light firepower (especially in anti-armor, air defense, and artillery), austere logistical support, and limited mobility, many feel these divisions would be hard pressed by even moderate mechanised forces, especially when external logistical support is provided solely by airlink as envisioned. Provisions are made to fly or ship-in heavy forces, usually in the form of armored or mech. brigades to support these contingency operations. Others also question the need for so many light divisions (four AC, one ARNG), especially given the existence of three other types of light divisions.

The 82nd Airborne Div. is the Army's only fully parachute deliverable division. While some believe that parachute delivery is no longer a viable option, having been made obsolete by the helicopter, they fail to take into consideration that without nearby advance bases with secure airfields, helicopters cannot deliver a force. An airborne force can be flown halfway around the world and delivered to a trouble spot without the initial need for a friendly regional airfield. The 82nd's strength is 12,790 troops.

The 101st Airborne Div. (Air Assault) is a completely helicopter transportable force; fully one-third of its elements can be moved in one lift by organic helicopters. The division is designed to maintain a rapid tempo of operations over extended ranges and to operate in both low- and mid-intensity conflicts. Its strength is 15,370.

The 9th Inf. Div. (Motorized) is also a unique force relying on light, unarmored, high-speed vehicles mounting a variety of rapid fire weapons for combat power and mobility. It too can be deployed by airlift, but due to its cross-country mobility and heavier firepower, it is expected to have more staying power against opposing mechanised forces.

While each of the various types of light divisions have unique internal structures, weapons, and equipment, their base organisation is similar: HQ & HQ Company, Division; ADA Battalion; Engineer Combat Battalion; MI Battalion (CEWI); Signal Battalion; MP Company; Chemical Company.

The DIVARTYs consist of an HHB and three FA Battalions, each with three batteries of 6 × M102 or M119 105mm towed howitzers. A light infantry division may also have a 155mm howitzer battery with 8 × M198 towed pieces. The motorised division, however, has three battalions of 155mm towed howitzers and a mixed battalion with one SP MLRS and two 105mm towed batteries. The ADA Battalions have an HHB and three (two in light infantry) Gun/Stinger Batteries, each with 9 × M167 20mm Vulcan towed guns and 20 Stinger missile teams.

Light division DISCOMs consist of Supply and Transport, Maintenance, and Medical Battalions and an Aircraft Maintenance Company (Battalion in the 101st Abn. Div.). They operate on the FAST concept as H-series infantry divisions.

Each type of light division's aviation (cavalry) brigade is different:

Light Infantry	*Airborne*
Cav. Recon. Sdn.	Air Cav. Sdn.
Attack Hel. Bn.	Attack Hel. Bn.
Aslt. Hel. Co. (× 2)	Aslt. Hel. Co. (× 2)
Air Assault	*Motorised*
Air Cav. Sdn.	Cav. Recon. Sdn.
Attack Hel. Bn. (× 4)	Attack Hel. Bn.
Aslt. Hel. Bn. (× 2)	Command Avn. Bn.
Medium Hel. Bn.	
Command Avn. Bn.	

Light Infantry Battalions have an HHC and three Rifle Companies, while Airborne and Air Assault Infantry Battalions also have an Anti-armor Company, with 20 × M220A1 wheeled vehicle-mounted TOWs in five platoons. The Rifle Companies have an HQ, a mortar section with 2 × 60mm M224s, and three rifle platoons of three squads. Platoon crew-served weapons include two each M60 MGs and Dragon missile systems in the HQ. The battalion mortar platoons in the HHC have 4 × 81mm M29A1s or M252s. Most Light Infantry Battalion leaders, officer and NCO, are required to be Ranger-qualified.

The infantry battalions of the 9th Inf. Div. are of three types. The five Light Combined Arms (CA) Battalions consist of an HHC, three Light CA Companies, and a CSC with all elements transported in high mobility, multipurpose wheeled vehicles

(HMMWV—'Hum-vee') mounting 25mm M242 'chain guns', 40mm MK 19-3 automatic grenade launchers, or M220A1 TOWs. The two Heavy CA Battalions are the same, but add an Assault Gun Company giving the battalion a total of 40 TOWs. The two Light Attack Battalions have an HHC and three Light Attack Companies smaller than the Motorized Infantry Companies.

Force Structure

The deployment, rôles, and recent histories (since Vietnam) of the Active and RC formations and units provides an overall perspective of the Army's missions:

The Armies
The numbered armies are assigned either supervisory responsibility of RC unit training within the continental US or administer specific combat formations:

First US Army Headquartered at Ft. George G. Meade, Md., it supervises RC units in the north-eastern US.

Second US Army This Ft. Gillem, Ga., command supervises RC units in the south-eastern US.

Third US Army Reactivated in 1983 and headquartered at Ft. McPherson, Ga., the Third

A tripod-mounted AN/TVQ-2 ground-vehicle laser locater-designator is aimed at a target to guide either a Hellfire missile or Copperhead 155mm projectile.

controls the Army component of the multi-service US Central Command (CENCOM), formerly the Rapid Deployment Force (RDF). Its principal formation is XVIII Abn. Corps and is targeted at south-west Asia.

Fourth US Army Headquartered at Ft. Sheridan, Ill., the Fourth supervises RC units in the north central US.

Fifth US Army With its headquarters at Ft. Sam Houston, Tex., the Fifth supervises RC units in the south central US.

Sixth US Army From its Presidio of San Francisco, Calif., headquarters the Sixth supervises RC units in the western US.

Seventh Army Based in Germany since 1950, the Seventh Army has been the principal combat force of US Army, Europe. Headquartered in Heidel-

berg, the Seventh commands V and VII Corps.

Eighth Army The Eighth has been in Korea since 1950 and was tasked with the command of all allied forces there until 1978 when the Korean/US Combined Forces Command was formed. Eighth Army then became subordinate to it to command US forces only. However, the Eighth Army commander also doubles as commander-in-chief of the United Nations Command. It is headquartered in Seoul.

The Corps

It surprises some that with the number of Active and RC divisions and separate brigades, and the importance of the corps as a tactical command and control formation, there are only six in the force structure. There are provisions to form more during a prolonged conflict, but some key resources, i.e. major combat support and combat service support units, are limited:

An M109A3 155mm howitzer crew loads an HE round. Note the MILES detector bands on their helmets.

I Corps 'Eye' Corps had been stationed in Korea since 1950 and was redesignated I Corps (Group) in 1955. Reduced to zero strength in 1980, it was replaced by the Korean/US Combined Field Army. Reorganised in 1981, I Corps was stationed at Ft. Lewis, Wash., and tasked with Pacific region contingency missions. Its secondary mission is to reinforce NATO. A large number of its combat support and combat service support units are provided by the RC.

III Corps The III Mobile Armored Corps (unofficial designation) has been based at Ft. Hood, Tex. since 1961. Its principal mission is to perform as the NATO Allied Central Europe Reserve Corps, i.e. to airlift its forces to Europe, draw pre-positioned heavy equipment, and conduct a major counterattack. To accomplish this the 'Phantom Corps' maintains several support organisations in Europe.

V Corps Headquartered in Frankfurt-am-Main since 1952, V Corps is responsible for the northern portion of Seventh Army's sector.

VII Corps Also in Germany since the 1950s, VII Corps is assigned the southern portion of Seventh Army's sector. It is headquartered in Stuttgart.

IX Corps Principally an 'administrative' corps, IX Corps has served as a component of the Ryukyus Command on Okinawa and was later merged with US Army, Japan. Now at Camp Zama, Japan, it is responsible for various logistical functions and western Pacific contingency planning, as well as supervising RC units in the Pacific through its IX Corps (Reinforcement) element at Ft. DeRussy, Hawaii.

XVIII Abn. Corps Based at Ft. Bragg, NC since 1951, the 'Dragon Corps' has performed as the

An M109A3 self-propelled 155mm howitzer moves into firing position at the National Training Center. This weapon is the mainstay of armored and mechanized infantry divisional artillery battalions.

The M270 multiple-Launch Rocket System is mounted on the M987 armoured carrier, a variant of the Bradley fighting vehicle chassis. Camouflage nets are stowed on the crew compartment.

principal command for the Army's strategic reaction force since 1958; whether it was called Strategic Army Corps, Army Strike Command, Rapid Deployment Force, or Central Command. The corps is prepared to commit forces worldwide.

The Divisions

Each of the Active divisions is structured for its specific mission and projected area of operations. Unless otherwise stated, each has three brigades:

1st Inf. Div. (Mech) The 'Big Red One' returned from Vietnam to its traditional home at Ft. Riley, Kans. and was upgraded to a mechanised unit by redesignating and utilising the assets of the 24th Inf. Div. Though aligned with III Corps for training, the division maintains a large element—1st Inf. Div. (Forward)—in Goppingen, Germany in the VII Corps sector. It is a key reinforcement unit for NATO's Central Army Group. It has recently begun to receive M1 tanks.

2nd Inf. Div. Stationed in Korea since 1964, the 'Indian Head Division' is the sole US division under Eighth Army's Combined Field Army (ROK/US). Headquartered at Camp Casey, Tongduchon along with its 1st Bde., its 2nd Bde. is located at nearby Camp Hovey. These forces sit astride one of the principal invasion routes to Seoul; the 3rd Bde. at Kaesong-Munsan straddles the other. Because of its key location the division acts as an effective deterrent to North Korea's aggressive tendencies. While considered a heavy division, the 2nd is actually a mixed force with three infantry and two each mech. and tank battalions. The latter replaced their M48A5 tanks with the M60A3TTS in 1985.

3rd Inf. Div. (Mech) Stationed in Germany since the 1950s, the 'Marne Division' is subordinate to VII Corps. Headquarterd in Wurzburg, the division's tank battalions are still in the process of receiving M1A1 tanks, but it was the first division to be fully outfitted with Bradley fighting vehicles.

4th Inf. Div. (Mech) After serving in Vietnam the 'Ivy Division' was reformed at Ft. Carson, Colo. (by redesignating the existing 5th Inf. Div.). It maintained a 4th Bde.—4th Inf. Div. (Forward)—in Wiesbaden, Germany until 1984 when it was disbanded under the J-series TOE reorganisation. The 5th is another division aligned with III Corps for training, but tasked with a NATO Central Army Group reinforcement rôle. It is still equipped with M60A3TTS tanks and M113 APCs.

5th Inf. Div. (Mech) Reactivated in 1975 at Ft. Polk, La., the 'Red Diamond Division' had been represented in Vietnam by its 1st Bde. The division's two Active brigades are rounded out by the Louisiana ARNG's 256th Inf. Bde. The 5th is attached to III Corps and shares its Allied Forces Central Europe reinforcement mission. It is equipped with M60A3TTS tanks and M113 APCs.

6th Inf. Div. (Lt) The 'Sightseeing Sixth' was last active from 1967–68 at Ft. Campbell, Ky. It was reactivated in 1986 with the HQ and 1st Bde. at Ft. Richardson, Alaska, using the assets of the 172nd Inf. Bde. (Sep). Its 2nd Bde. will form at Ft. Wainwright, Alaska in 1988–89. Its roundout brigade is the USAR's 205th Inf. Bde. Attached to I Corps, it is the principal ground combat force of Task Force Alaska.

7th Inf. Div. (Lt) Stationed in Korea until the early 1970s, the 'Bayonet Division' was reactivated at Ft. Ord, Calif., in 1978 as a low priority two-brigade unit. Its status changed in 1984 when it began reorganisation as the Army's first light infantry division; now with three brigades, it has the highest priority of the light divisions. Attached to I Corps, it trains for employment in potential low-intensity conflict regions.

8th Inf. Div. (Mech) Long stationed in Germany, the 'Golden Arrow Division' is headquartered at Bad Kreuznach and attached to V Corps. The division is still equipped with M60A3TTS tanks and M113 APCs, but will soon replace them.

9th Inf. Div. (Motorized) The 'Old Reliables' returned from Vietnam, where they had pioneered

Active Army Divisions' Subordinate Combat Units

Division	Maneuver Battalions	Cav. Sdn.	FA Bns.	FA Btys.	ADA Bn.	Engr. Bn.
1st Inf. (Mech.)	1–16 Inf. (M), 2–16 Inf. (M), 4–16 Inf. (M), 5–16 Inf. (M), 1–34 Arm., 2–34 Arm., 3–37 Arm., 4–37 Arm.	1–4	1–1 (155 SP), 2–5 (155 SP), 4–5 (155 SP)	A-6 (MLRS), D-25 (TA)	2–3	1
2nd Inf.	1–5 Inf. (M), 5–20 Inf. (M), 1–503 Inf. (L), 2–503 Inf. (L), 1–506 Inf. (L), 1–72 Arm., 2–72 Arm.	4–17 (Air)	1–4 (155 T), 8–8 (155 T), 1–15 (155 SP), 6–37 (203/MLRS)	E-25 (TA)	5–5	2
3rd Inf. (Mech.)	1–7 Inf. (M), 4–7 Inf. (M), 1–15 Inf. (M), 2–15 Inf. (M), 5–15 Inf. (M), 2–64 Arm., 3–64 Arm., 4–66 Arm., 1–69 Arm., 4–69 Arm.	4–4	2–41 (155 SP), 1–10 (155 SP), 2–39 (155 SP)	A-25 (TA), A-94 (MLRS)	4–3	10
4th Inf. (Mech.)	1–8 Inf. (M), 2–8 Inf. (M), 1–12 Inf. (M), 2–12 Inf. (M), 2–35 Arm., 3–68 Arm., 4–68 Arm., 1–77 Arm., 2–77 Arm.	2–7	1–29 (155 SP), 3–29 (155 SP), 5–29 (155 SP)	C-10 (MLRS), H-29 (TA)	1–3	4
5th Inf. (Mech.)	3–6 Inf. (M), 4–6 Inf. (M), 5–6 Inf. (M), 4–35 Arm., 1–70 Arm., 3–70 Arm.	3–1	3–19 (155 SP), 2–21 (155 SP)	C-21 (MLRS), H-25 (TA)	3–3	7
6th Inf. (Lt.)	1–9 Inf. (L), 5–9 Inf. (L), 6–9 Inf. (L), 1–17 Inf. (L), 4–505 (Abn.) (not all division elements are yet formed)	4–9 (Recon.)	4–11 (105 T), 5–11 (105 T)	E-11 (155 T)	4–62	96
7th Inf. (Lt.)	2–9 Inf. (L), 3–9 Inf. (L), 4–9 Inf. (L), 3–17 Inf. (L), 4–17 Inf. (L), 4–21 Inf. (L), 2–37 Inf. (L), 3–37 Inf. (L)	2–9 (Recon.)	2–8 (105 T), 6–8 (105 T), 7–15 (105 T)	B-15 (155 T)	2–62	13
8th Inf. (Mech.)	3–8 Inf. (M), 4–8 Inf. (M), 5–8 Inf. (M), 3–12 Inf. (M), 4–12 Inf. (M), 3–34 Arm., 1–68 Arm., 2–68 Arm., 3–77 Arm., 5–77 Arm.	3–7	2–29 (155 SP), 4–29 (155 SP), 6–29 (155 SP)	C-16 (MLRS), C-333 (TA)	5–3	12
9th Inf. (Mtz.)	2–1 Inf. (LA), 3–1 Inf. (HCA), 2–2 Inf. (LCA), 2–23 Inf. (LCA), 4–23 Inf. (LCA), 2–47 Inf. (LCA), 3–47 Inf. (LCA), 2–60 Inf. (HCA), 3–60 Inf. (LA)	1–9 (Recon.)	1–11 (155 T), 3–11 (155 T), 6–11 (155 T), 1–84 (105 T/MLRS)	E-333 (TA)	1–4	15
10th Mt. (Lt. Inf.)	2–14 Inf. (L), 3–14 Inf. (L), 1–22 Inf. (L), 2–22 Inf. (L), 1–87 Inf. (L), 2–87 Inf. (L) (not all division elements are yet formed)	3–17 (Recon.)	1–7 (105 T), 2–7 (105 T)		1–5	126
24th Inf. (Mech.)	2–7 Inf. (M), 3–7 Inf. (M), 3–15 Inf. (M), 1–64 Arm., 4–64 Arm., 3–69 Arm.	2–4	1–35 (155 SP), 2–35 (155 SP)	A-13 (MLRS)	1–5	3
25th Inf. (Lt.)	1–14 Inf. (L), 5–14 Inf. (L), 1–21 Inf. (L), 2–21 Inf. (L), 3–22 Inf. (L), 4–22 Inf. (L), 1–27 Inf. (L), 4–27 Inf. (L), 4–87 Inf. (L)	5–9 (Recon.)	3–7 (105 T), 7–8 (105 T), 2–11 (105 T)		1–62	65

Table continued overleaf

Division	Maneuver Battalions	Cav. Sdn.	FA Bns.	FA Btys.	ADA Bn.	Engr. Bn.
82nd Abn.	1–325 Inf., 2–325 Inf., 3–325 Inf., 1–504 Inf., 2–504 Inf., 3–504 Inf., 1–505 Inf., 2–505 Inf., 3–505 Inf. (all are Abn.)	1–17 (Air)	1–319 (105 T), 2–319 (105 T), 3–319 (105 T)	1 FA Det (TA)	3–4	307
101st Abn. (Air Aslt.)	1–187 Inf., 3–187 Inf., 4–187 Inf., 1–327 Inf., 2–327 Inf., 3–327 Inf., 1–502 Inf., 3–503 Inf., (all are Air Aslt.), C–509 Inf. (Pathfinder)	2–17 (Air)	1–320 (105 T), 2–320 (105 T), 3–320 (105 T)		8–4	326
1st Cav.	1–5 Cav. (M), 2–5 Cav. (M), 1–8 Cav. (Tk), 2–8 Cav. (Tk), 1–32 Arm., 2–32 Arm.	1–7	1–82 (155 SP), 3–82 (155 SP)	A–21 (MLRS), A–333 (TA)	4–5	8
1st Armd.	1–6 Inf. (M), 2–6 Inf. (M), 6–6 Inf. (M), 7–6 Inf. (M), 1–35 Arm., 3–35 Arm., 1–37 Arm., 2–37 Arm., 2–70 Arm., 4–70 Arm.	1–1	6–14 (155 SP), 1–22 (155 SP), 2–28 (155 SP)	A–94 (MLRS), A–25 (TA)	6–3	16
2nd Armd.	1–41 Inf. (M), 2–41 Inf. (M), 3–41 Inf. (M), 4–41 Inf. (M), 1–66 Arm., 2–66 Arm., 3–66 Arm., 1–67 Arm., 3–67 Arm.	2–1	1–3 (155 SP), 3–3 (155 SP), 4–3 (155 SP)	A–92 (MLRS), G–29 (TA)	2–5	17
3rd Armd.	4–18 (M), 5–18 (M), 3–5 Cav. (M), 5–5 Cav. (M), 3–8 Cav. (Tk), 4–8 Cav. (Tk), 2–32 Arm., 3–32 Arm., 2–67 Arm., 4–67 Arm.	4–7	2–3 (155 SP), 2–6 (155 SP), 2–75 (155 SP)	A–40 (MLRS), F–333 (TA)	3–5	23

Note: Certain 1st Cav. and 3rd Armd. Div. mechanized infantry and tank battalions carry cavalry lineages and are so designated.
CA—Combined Arms, LA—Light Attack, H—Heavy, L—Light, M—Mechanized, MLRS—Multiple Launch Rocket System, SP—Self Propelled, T—Towed, TA—Targert Acquisition, Tk—Tank

the riverine concept, and were stationed at Ft. Lewis, Wash. They soon pioneered another unique concept when designated the High-Technology Light Division. Placing heavy reliance on light, high-speed wheeled vehicles and advanced electronic command, control, communications and intelligence systems, the division went through extensive testing and a number of internal reorganisations. In 1984 its organisation and techniques of operation were standardised and it was redesignated the Army's only motorised division, though its equipment development continues. It is attached to I Corps.

10th Mountain Div. (Lt Inf) Formed in the Second World War as the Army's only mountain division, the 'Mountaineers' had not been active since the early 1950s (serving as the 10th Inf. Div.). Reactivated in 1984, its HQ and 1st Bde. are at Ft. Drum, NY, and the 2nd Bde. at Ft. Benning, Ga. (scheduled to relocate to Ft. Drum in 1989). Its roundout brigade is the New York ARNG's 27th Inf. Bde. The 10th carries the 'Mountain' title as a traditional designation, but is organised as a standard light infantry unit. It is attached to XVIII Abn. Corps.

24th Inf. Div. (Mech) The 'Victory Division' was stationed in Germany until it relocated to Ft. Riley, Kansas in 1968 as part of NATO troop reductions, and inactivated in 1970. It was reactivated at Ft. Stewart, Ga. in 1975; now attached to XVIII Abn. Corps, it is the principal heavy division of Third US Army. With two brigades, its roundout is provided by the Georgia ARNG's 48th Inf. Bde. The 24th is fully equipped with M1 tanks and received Bradley M2A1 infantry and M3A1 cavalry fighting vehicles in 1988.

1: Drill Sergeant
2: Physical training suit
3: Basic trainee
4: Female Drill Sergeant

THIS WE'LL DEFEND

A

Light Infantry Fire Team, 7th Inf. Div. (Lt.), Ft. Ord, California:
1: Sgt. team leader
2: Grenadier
3: SAW gunner
4: Rifleman

B   4   3   1   2

1: Stinger AA missile system; 2nd Armd. Div.
2: M47 Dragon missile system; 8th Inf. Div. (Mech.)
3: M224 60mm mortar; 82nd Abn. Div.

C

1: Cold-Wet Uniform;
   2nd Inf. Div., S. Korea
2: Cold-Dry Uniform;
   6th Inf. Div. (Lt.), Alaska

4

1

3

2

3: Extended Cold Weather
   system; 10th Mtn. Div.
4: Snow camouflage;
   25th Inf. Div. (Lt.) Japan

D

1: Desert BDU, 101st Abn. Div.; UN MFO, Egypt
2: Lightweight BDU; 1169th Eng. Gp., Ecuador

3: Rain suit; 5th Inf. Div. (Mech.)
4: Desert Night Camouflage Uniform; 24th Inf. Div.
   (Mech.), Egypt

E

1: MOPP 4
2: M25A1 Tank Protective Mask

3: XM40 Protective Mask
4: Bomb Disposal Clothing System

F

1: CWU-27/P Flyer's Coverall; 6th Cav. Bde.
2: MA-1 Intermediate Flyer's Jacket; 1st Armd. Div.
3: N-2B Cold Weather Flyer's Jacket
4: SPH-4 Flight Helmet, SRU-21/P Survival Vest

G

1: TC, l94th Armd. Bde. (Sep.)
2: OPFOR soldier, 60th Gds. Mot. Rifle Div.
3: Mechanic's Coverall
4: Tank bn. CO, 32nd Gds. Mot. Rifle Regt., OPFOR

H

2

1,2: Infantrymen, c.1990
3: Sniper 'ghillie suit';
   7th Inf. Div. (Lt.)

1

3

VOISTAD

I

1: Officer's Army Green Uniform, Class A; 1st Inf. Div. (Mech.)
2: Enlisted Army Green Uniform, 4th US Army
3: Enlisted Pullover Sweater; 7th Tspt. Gp.
4: Officer's Windbreaker

J

1
2
3

VOLSTAD

HONOR GUARD

1: Enlisted Army Blue Uniform; Guard, Tomb of the Unknown
   Soldier, Arlington
2: Officer's Army Blue Uniform
3: General Officer's Army Blue Uniform

K

1: Officer's Army White Mess Uniform
2: Officer's Army Blue Evening Mess Uniform
3: General Officer's Army Blue Uniform & Cape

L

Active Army Brigades' Subordinate Units

Brigade	Maneuver Battalions	FA Bn./Bty.	Cav. Trp.	Engr. Co.	Spt. Bn.	Misc. Units
177th Armd. (Sep.)	1–52 Inf. (M), 1–63 Arm., 1–33 Arm. (to be added later)			87 (H)	177	177 MI Co. Smoke Plat
193rd Inf. (Panama)	5–87 Inf. (L), 4–504 Inf. (L) (Co A/4–504 Inf. is Abn.)	D–320 (105 T)		518	193	193 MI Co. 396 Sig. Co.
194th Armd. (Sep.)	1–10 Cav. (Tk), 2–10 Cav. (Tk) 4–15 Inf. (M)	1–77 (155 SP)	D–10	522	75	160 Chem Plat. 217 Chem Det.
197th Inf. (Mech.) (Sep.)	1–18 Inf. (M), 2–18 Inf. (M), 2–69 Arm.	2–10 (155 SP)	F–4	72	197	197 MI Det. 187 Inf. Det.
Berlin	4–502 Inf., 5–502 Inf., 6–502 Inf. (all are Light)	E–320 (155 SP)				F–40 Arm. (Tk)

Separate infantry battalions also exist:
1–3 Inf.—Military District of Washington
2–4 Inf. (M)—56th Arty. Command, Germany
4–31 Inf. (M)—III Corps Arty., Ft. Still, Okla.
4–325 Inf. (Abn.)—Southern European Task Force, Italy (includes D–319 FA (105 T))

25th Inf. Div. (Lt) The 'Tropic Lightning' returned from Vietnam to its previous post at Schofield Barracks, Hawaii, reassuming its former Pacific strategic reaction force rôle. It was reorganised as a light infantry division in 1985. Originally consisting of two brigades, it was rounded out by the Hawaii ARNG's 29th Inf. Bde., until it received a 3rd Bde. in 1986. The 25th is subordinate to Western Command, but also may operate with I Corps.

82nd Abn. Div. The 'All Americans' have long been stationed at Ft. Bragg, NC functioning as the Army's 'fire brigade', serving in the Dominican Republic (1964), Vietnam (3rd Bde. only, 1968–69), and Grenada (1983). The 82nd is attached to XVIII Abn. Corps and is prepared for worldwide deployment.

101st Abn. Div. (Air Assault) The 'Screaming Eagles' are no longer an airborne (parachute delivered) unit, but retain the title as a traditional designation. Converted to an airmobile division in 1968 while in Vietnam, it returned to its former home at Ft. Campbell, Ky., and was redesignated 'Air Assault' in 1977. Now the Army's only air assault division, it is attached to XVIII Abn. Corps.

1st Cav. Div. Having pioneered the airmobile concept, the 'First Team' relocated from Vietnam to Ft. Hood, Tex., to take part in the development of another tactical innovation, the early 1970s Triple Capability (TRICAP) concept: a mix of armor, mech. and airmobile infantry, and attack helicopter units. The tests were not entirely successful, but they did have benefits, to include the eventual formation of divisional aviation brigades. Attached to III Corps, in 1974 it began conversion to a standard armored division. It lost its 3rd Bde. in 1983 and now has the Mississippi ARNG's 155th Armd. Bde. as a roundout. The 'Cav' is fully equipped with M1 tanks and Bradley fighting vehicles.

1st Armd. Div. 'Old Ironsides' had been stationed at Ft. Hood since returning from Germany in 1946. Its assets were used to reform the 1st Cav. Div. in 1970–71 while the 4th Armd. Div. in Germany was redesignated the 1st in 1971. Headquartered at Ansbach, it is attached to VII Corps. The division is in the process of being equipped with M1 tanks and Bradley fighting vehicles.

2nd Armd. Div. The 'Hell on Wheels' division has been at Ft. Hood since returning from Germany in 1946. Attached to III Corps, it also maintains the

2nd Armd. Div. (Forward) in Garlstedt, Germany. This provides III Corps with an in-place force on the North German Plain, establishing a US presence astride this key invasion route. Now with three brigades, the division formerly maintained four (the 4th was in Germany). The division was the first to be fully equipped with M1 tanks and Bradley fighting vehicles.

3rd Armd. Div. The 'Spearhead Division' has been stationed in Germany since the 1950s. Headquartered at Frankfurt-am-Main, it is attached to V Corps. It is in the process of being equipped with M1 tanks and Bradley fighting vehicles.

All ARNG divisions have three brigades, many of which carry the designation of former divisions or the old 1917–41 divisional brigades. It is not uncommon for the divisions' elements to be located in two or more states:

26th Inf. Div. The 'Yankee Division' is headquartered in Boston, Mass., the same state as its 1st and 3rd Bdes. Its 43rd Bde. is in Connecticut.

28th Inf. Div. Located entirely in Pennsylvania, the 'Keystone Division' is headquartered in Harrisburg and consists of the 2nd, 55th and 56th Bdes.

29th Inf. Div. (Lt) Formed in 1985 as the ARNG's only light division, the 'Blue and Gray Division' has its HQ at Ft. Belvoir, Va. Its 1st and 2nd (former 116th Inf. Bde.) Bdes. are also in Virginia and the 3rd (former 58th Inf. Bde.) in Maryland. Some of its elements are not yet fully formed.

35th Inf. Div. (Mech) Reformed in 1984 as the first ARNG division to be organised under the J-series TOE, the 'Santa Fe Division' is headquartered at Ft. Levenworth, Kansas. All of its brigades were former separate units and are located as follows: 67th—Nebraska, 69th—Kansas, 149th—Kentucky. The 69th was federalised and attached to the 5th Inf. Div. in 1968–69 while its 1st Bde. was in Vietnam. Many of the 35th's support units are located in other states and are still in the process of forming. It is aligned with III Corps.

Both systems making up the counter-battery Firefinder radars are pictured here. The larger AN/TPQ-37 is used for artillery locating, while the AN/TPQ-36 locates mortars. They are connected to artillery unit fire direction centres by datalink and can pass near-real-time targeting information.

38th Inf. Div. Headquartered in Indianapolis, Ind., the 'Cyclone Division' consists of the 2nd and 76th Bdes., located in the same state, with the 46th Bde. in Michigan.

40th Inf. Div. (Mech) One of two ARNG divisions to see combat in Korea, the 'Grizzly Division' has since been organised as a separate brigade and later as an armored division. Its 1st, 2nd and 3rd Bdes. are all in California with its HQ located at Naval Air Station Los Alamitos.

42nd Inf. Div. The 'Rainbow Division' is located entirely in New York and consists of the 1st, 2nd and 3rd Bdes; the latter is still forming after the 27th Bde. was made separate in 1987. The HQ is New York City.

47th Inf. Div. The 'Viking Division' has its HQ in St. Paul, Minn., with its brigades in different states: 1st—Minnesota, 34th—Iowa, 66th—Illinois. It is now aligned with I Corps and principally tasked to support Task Force Alaska.

49th Armd. Div. The 'largest division in NATO', the 'Lonestar Division' is headquartered in Austin, Tex. It consists of the 1st, 2nd and 3rd Bdes., all in Texas and is aligned with III Corps. It was one of the two ARNG divisions Federalised during the 1961 Berlin crisis.

50th Armd. Div. The 'Jersey Blues' are headquartered in Somerset, NJ, with its 1st and 2nd Bdes. in the same state. Its 83rd Bde. is located in Vermont, but at the time of writing it is planned for it to be reassigned to Texas where it may be redesignated the 36th, but will remain assigned to the 50th Div.

The Separate Brigades

The few Active separate brigades are tasked with specific missions:

177th Armd. Bde. (Sep) Formed in 1986 from former 7th Inf. Div. elements based at the National Training Center, Ft. Erwin, Calif., it has continued its same mission of manning the OPFOR 60th Motorised Rifle Div. (-). Equipped with M1 tanks, it also has a combat mission.

193rd Inf. Bde. (Panama) Stationed at Ft. Clayton with some of its elements at Ft. Kobbe, this unit has undergone a number of internal reorganisations over the years. It is subordinate to US Army, South and tasked with defence of the Panama Canal.

194th Armd. Bde. (Sep) Originally employed as an experimentation and support unit for the Armor

The improved CH-47D Chinook, with greatly increased lift and range, equips Assault Support and Medium Cargo Helicopter Battalions. This one sling-loads six 500 gal. fuel bladders. It can also lift the M198 155mm howitzer.

School, it was given a combat mission in 1975 and tasked to support XVIII Abn. Corps.

197th Inf. Bde. (Mech) (Sep) The 197th 'Forever Forward' brigade originally supported the Infantry School, but was given a combat mission in 1973 and tasked to support XVIII Abn. Corps.

Berlin Bde. Based in West Berlin, this 'forward deployed' unit was a provisional force until placed under a formal TOE in 1983. It is subordinate to the US Command Berlin.

ARNG and USAR separate brigades may be intended as roundout units for two-brigade Active divisions or may be assigned specific wartime tasks. Some carry former division designations and others those of the old brigades. All are ARNG unless identified as USAR:

27th Inf. Bde. (Sep) Formerly part of the 42nd Inf. Div., the 'New Yorkers' were made a separate brigade in 1987 to serve as a roundout for the 10th Mountain Div., but has not yet reorganised as light infantry. Its HQ is in Syracuse.

An M60 machine gunner and his assistant prepare to enter a building during MOUT training. Both are outfitted with MILES gear.

29th Inf. Bde. (Sep) This first RC combat brigade was federalised in 1968–69, but remained in Hawaii assuming the 11th Inf. Bde.'s Pacific reaction force mission after the former deployed to Vietnam. Headquartered in Honolulu, it has elements throughout the islands. From 1973 to 1986 it was the roundout brigade of the 25th Inf. Div., and still trains with it. The brigade itself has a roundout unit in the form of the USAR's 100th Bn., 442nd Inf.[1]

30th Inf. Bde. (Mech) (Sep) Stationed in Clinton, NC, the 'Old Hickory' brigade is tasked with a European mission and equipped with M1 tanks and M2 IFVs.

30th Armd. Bde. (Sep) Headquartered in Jackson,

Tenn., the 'Volunteers' are tasked with a European mission.

31st Armd. Bde. (Sep) The 'Dixie' brigade is stationed in Northport, Ala. and is aligned with the 5th Inf. Div. for training. It too has a European mission.

32nd Inf. Bde. (Mech) (Sep) The 'Red Arrows' are headquartered in Milwaukee, Wisc. and are assigned the mission of supporting the Alaska ARNG's 207th Inf. Gp. In 1961, as a division, it was federalised during the Berlin crisis.

33rd Inf. Bde. (Sep) Headquartered in Chicago, Ill., the 'Prairie' brigade was used on two occasions to quell major civil disturbances during the turmoil of the late 1960s. It is now tasked to support the Infantry School in event of mobilisation.

39th Inf. Bde. (Sep) The 'Arkansas Brigade' trains to reinforce the 101st Abn. Div. Its HQ is in Little Rock.

41st Inf. Bde. (Sep) Tasked as a roundout for the

[1]100th/442nd Inf. carries the linage of two Second World War *nisei* (Japanese-American) units, 100th Inf. Bn. (Sep) and 442nd Inf. Regt., later consolidated into a single unit. The Battalion's Co. B is located on American Samoa.

7th Inf. Div. in the mid-1970s, the 41st lost that mission in 1985 when the division received a third brigade, but it still trains with the 7th and is aligned with I Corps. It is headquartered in Portland, Oregon.

45th Inf. Bde. (Sep) The 'Thunderbirds' was one of two ARNG divisions to see combat in Korea. Now an Edmonton, Okla. based brigade, it is tasked as III Corps' rear battle force.

48th Inf. Bde. (Mech) (Sep) As the 24th Inf. Div.'s. roundout brigade since 1976, the 48th was the first RC unit to rotate through the National Training Center. Equipped with M1 tanks and M2 IFVs, it is stationed in Macon, Ga.

53rd Inf. Bde. (Sep) Headquartered in Tampa, Fla., the 53rd has the mobilisation mission of augmenting the 193rd Inf. Bde. in Panama.

73rd Inf. Bde (Sep) The 73rd is tasked with a wartime rear battle mission in Europe. Its HQ is in Columbus, Ohio.

81st Inf. Bde. (Mech) (Sep) Headquartered in Seattle, Wash., the 81st is aligned with the 9th Inf. Div. for training. It was used for the 1980 clean-up after the Mount St. Helens' eruption.

92nd Inf. Bde. (Sep) Tasked with the defence of the Caribbean basin, the 92nd has also conducted civil disturbance and disaster relief missions in the region. In 1980 and 1981, when it deployed to Costa Rica, it was the first ARNG unit to provide disaster relief outside the continental US. Its HQ is in San Juan, Puerto Rico.

155th Armd. Bde. (Sep) From 1980–83 the 155th was the 5th Inf. Div.'s roundout. It was then tasked as the roundout for the 1st Cav. Div., and as such was the first ARNG brigade to be fully equipped with M1 tanks and Bradley IFVs. Its HQ is in Tupelo, Miss.

157th Inf. Bde. (Mech) (Sep) This USAR brigade is headquartered in Horsham, Pa., but some elements are in New Jersey.

187th Inf. Bde. (Sep) The 187th, also a USAR unit, is headquartered at Ft. Devens, Mass., but also has units in Maine, New Hampshire, New York, and Pennsylvania. It is tasked to deploy either to Iceland or Europe, as required, for its wartime mission.

205th Inf. Bde. (Lt) (Sep) This USAR unit is the roundout for the 6th Inf. Div. in Alaska, and as such is the first USAR unit to receive a roundout mission.

Headquartered at Ft. Snelling, Minn., it also has some units in Iowa and Wisconsin.

207th Inf. Gp. (Scout) While the ARNG's 'Arctic Warriors' is not a brigade, it is of similar size and the only infantry group in the Army. Headquartered in Anchorage, Alaska, the unit has both mech. and scout infantry battalions. The three scout battalions patrol Alaska's extensive rugged coastline facing the Soviet Union.

218th Inf. Bde. (Mech) (Sep) Headquartered in Newberry, SC, the 218th is aligned for training with the 24th Inf. Div.

256th Inf. Bde. (Mech) (Sep) In 1983 the 256th was tasked as the roundout for the 5th Inf. Div. Its HQ is in Lafayette, La.

The Armored Cavalry Regiments

The Active ACRs are attached to specific corps:

2nd ACR Headquartered in Nurnberg, Germany, the 'Second Dragons' are attached to VII Corps' Border Command. It has been in Germany since 1958 and is equipped with M1 tanks.

3rd ACR Based at Ft. Bliss, Tex., the 'Brave Rifles' are attached to III Corps. It has been at Ft. Bliss since 1972, having moved there from Ft. Lewis,

The business end of the M901 improved TOW vehicle (ITV). Between the two TOW tubes are the target acquisition and sighting systems. The M981 fire support team vehicle (FIST-V) is similar, with the sensor pod even disguised to appear as a TOW turret.

Infantrymen, wearing ALICE load carrying equipment, co-ordinate with a supporting M901 ITV's commander. (Emerson Electric Co.)

Wash. It is the only stateside unit to be equipped with M1A1 tanks.

11th ACR The 'Blackhorse Regiment' served in Germany from 1957 to 1963 until the 6th ACR at Ft. George G. Meade, Md., was redesignated the 11th. In 1966 the 11th deployed to Vietnam, where it remained until returning to the US in 1971. The next year the 14th ACR in Germany was redesignated the 11th. Based in Fulda and equipped with M1 tanks, the 11th is attached to V Corps providing border security.

The ARNG ACRs are also assigned corps missions:

107th ACR Headquartered in Cleveland, Ohio, the same state as its 2nd and 3rd Sdns.; its other squadron is 1st/150th ACR in West Virginia. It is tasked with a European mission.

116th ACR The 'Snake River Regiment' has its HQ in Twin Falls, Idaho. Its squadrons are: 1st/108th—Mississippi, 2nd/116th—Idaho, 3rd/116th—Oregon. It is tasked to support I Corps.

163rd ACR The 'First Montana' is headquartered in Bozeman, Mont. with its 1st and 2nd Sdns.; the 3rd Sdn. is in Texas. The 163rd is aligned with the 3rd ACR for training and has a European mission.

278th ACR The 'Three Rivers Regiment' has its

HQ in Knoxville, Tenn., the same state in which all of its squadrons are based. It is aligned with the 24th Inf. Div. for training and tasked to support XVIII Abn. Corps.

Combat Support Brigades
FA Brigades—9 AC, 18 ARNG, 3 USAR
ADA Brigades—2 AC, 2 ARNG
Engineer Brigades—3 AC, 4 ARNG, 2 USAR
MP Brigades—3 AC, 4 ARNG, 2 USAR
MI Brigades (CEWI)—5 AC
Aviation Brigades (Corps)—5 AC, 1 ARNG
Signal Brigades—5 AC, 3 ARNG, 1 USAR
Chemical Brigades—1 AC, 3 USAR

The Swedish-designed M973 small unit support vehicle was adopted by the Army in 1983 for use in far northern and arctic regions. The rear car is not a trailer, but a powered component of the vehicle.

1st Special Operations Command
Headquartered at Ft. Bragg, NC, 1st SOCOM became the Army component of the newly formed joint US Special Operations Command in May 1987. Its span of control includes the command of all AC special operations forces (SOFs), operational control of USAR SOFs, and monitoring the training and readiness of ARNG SOFs. Army SOFs include Special Forces (SF), Ranger, psychological operations (Psyops), and civil affairs (CA) units[1]:

1st SF Gp. (Abn.) Ft. Lewis, Wash., 1st Bn. on Okinawa

3rd SF Gp. (Abn.) To be formed at Ft. Bragg in 1989

5th SF Gp. (Abn.) Ft. Campbell, Ky.

[1]See Elite 4, *US Army Special Forces 1952–84* and Elite 13, *US Army Rangers and LRRP Units 1942–87*.

7th SF Gp. (Abn.) Ft. Bragg, 3rd Bn. in Panama
10th SF Gp. (Abn.) Ft. Devens, Mass., 1st Bn. in Germany
11th and 12th SF Gps. (Abn.) USAR
19th and 20th SF Gps. (Abn.) ARNG
75th Ranger Regt. HHC and 3rd Bn. at Ft. Benning, Ga.; 1st Bn. at Hunter Army Air Field, Ga.; 2nd Bn. at Ft. Lewis, Wash.
96th CA, 112th Signal, 528th Support Bns. (Abn.) Ft. Bragg
160th Aviation Spl. Opns. Gp. (Abn.) Ft. Campbell, Ky.
4th Psyops. Gp. (1st, 6th, 8th, 9th CA Bns.) Ft. Bragg
351st, 352nd and 353rd CA Commands USAR
358th and 361st CA Bdes. USAR

The Plates

A1: Drill Sergeant

Outfitted in the universally-worn battle dress uniform (BDU), this DS wears the drill sergeant's trademark, the 'Smokey Bear' hat, or officially 'hat, drill sergeant, male, enlisted'. Modelled after the M1910 campaign hat (used until 1942), its style led to the drill sergeants' nickname of 'Smokey Bear'—never uttered by trainees in their presence. He wears the Expert Infantryman's Badge and the cloth version of the metal Drill Sergeant Identification Badge.

A2: Physical Training Suit

Introduced in 1987, the physical training suit replaces a reversible gold-black version—the Army's colours; matching short-sleeve undershirt and running shorts are also available. These are not issued, but purchased from Quartermaster Sales. Running shoes are also privately purchased.

A3: Basic Trainee

Basic trainees wear a helmet liner with their company designation stencilled on the side; M1 steel helmets are also worn. Upon graduating to

The 40mm MK19-2 automatic grenade launcher is in use by the 9th Inf.Div., but will also be issued to MP units for their rear area protection rôle.

Military police helmets and liners are painted semi-gloss black with the 'MP' in white. The MP unit's insignia (or that of its parent formation) and designation are optional, but usually displayed. The stripes indicate the unit's level of assignment: Division units—1¼ in. red; Corps units—⅝ in. blue over ⅝ in. red; Army units—⅝ in. white over ⅝ in. red; all other MP units—1¼ in. white.

Advanced Individual Training, they are permitted to wear camouflage covers to set them apart from basic trainees. The brown AS 436 undershirt has completely replaced the olive green OG 109 for wear with all field, or Class C uniforms.

A4: Female Drill Sergeant

With the increase in female volunteers in the mid-1970s, female DSs were authorised their own distinctive hat.

B: Light Infantry Fire Team; 7th Infantry Division (Light), Ft. Ord, California

A rifle squad consists of two four-man fire teams, designated Alfa and Bravo, and a squad leader. One team provides a base of fire while the other maneuvers, and then rôles are switched. The staff sergeant squad leader, positioned between the two teams, directs the squad by verbal orders and arm and hand signals. The squad move with the fire team in wedges, with the rear team covering the lead. During contact the teams will alternate, bounding past each other and providing covering fire. One of the platoon's two 7.62mm M60 MG

teams may be attached to a squad and positioned near the squad leader. These troops are equipped with the Integrated Individual Fighting System, consisting of the Individual Tactical Load Bearing Vest and the new large field pack.[1] They also wear the Personal Armor System for Ground Troops (PASGT) helmet, commonly called the 'Fritz' due to its similarity to the German 'coal scuttle' design.

$B1$: The team leader, a sergeant, leads by example, i.e. his men freeze when he halts, fires when and where he does. He is armed with an M16A1 rifle. $B2$: The grenadier is armed with an M16A1 mounting a 40mm M203 grenade launcher. $B3$: The squad automatic weapon (SAW) gunner carries a 5.56mm M249E1 SAW with a 200-round belt in the assault magazine; it will also accept M16A1 magazines. $B4$: The rifleman is armed with an M16A1 rifle and carries a one-shot 66mm M72A3 light anti-tank weapon (LAW).

C1: Stinger Anti-Aircraft Missile System; 2nd Armored Division, Ft. Hood, Texas

The Stinger missile system, proved effective in Afghanistan and Nicaragua, is replacing the M41 Redeye as the small unit portable air defense weapon. It is issued as a round of ammunition in a disposable launch tube requiring no maintenance or testing. The 2nd Armd. Div. traditionally wears its 'Hell on Wheels' patch on the left chest—as Patton once stated that he wanted the division to be close to his men's hearts! A .45 cal. M1911A1 pistol is carried in the M11 shoulder holster.

C2: M47 Dragon Medium Anti-tank/Assault Missile System; 8th Infantry Division (Mechanized), West Germany

The wire-guided Dragon's 1,000m range and high hit probability provides rifle platoons with an unprecedented tank-kill capability. The missile is issued as a round of ammunition in its disposable launch tube. The Dragon is fitted with an AN/TAS-5 night tracker (sight) which detects a target's thermal (heat) signature. Its replacement, the Advanced Anti-tank Weapon System-Medium, is under development. This Specialist 4 is outfitted with the All-Purpose Lightweight Individual Carrying Equipment (ALICE), adopted in 1974 and still standard.

[1] See MAA 205, *US Army Combat Equipments 1910–1988*.

C3: M224 60mm Lightweight Mortar; 82nd Airborne Division, Ft. Bragg, North Carolina

Light, airborne, air assault and Ranger rifle companies' mortar sections are equipped with this excellent weapon to provide immediate indirect fire support. Its 3,500m range, coupled with greatly improved M720HE rounds, makes it almost as effective as the 81mm M29A1 mortar. This mortarman is armed with the new 9mm M9 pistol (Beretta 92 SB-F) in an M12 holster.

D1: Cold-Wet Uniform; 2nd Infantry Division, South Korea

This uniform is designed to protect against the wet snow, slush, rain, mud and changing temperatures of a cold-wet environment. It includes long underwear, olive green OG 108 wool shirt and trousers, woodlands pattern camouflage field jacket (which replaced the M65 OG 107 in 1987) and liner, and OG 107 field trousers. It was planned to issue camouflage field trousers, but this has not been undertaken. The black rubber insulated boots are exceptionally warm and waterproof. He carries an M1911A1 pistol in an M2 holster.

D2: Cold-Dry Uniform; 6th Infantry Division (Light), Ft. Richardson, Alaska

The cold-dry uniform protects against the temperature extremes, snow, ice and high winds found in far northern and arctic regions. It consists of the cold-wet uniform, with the addition of arctic parka and trousers, both with insulated liners. The camouflage-pattern insulated cap replaced the OG 107 type in the early 1980s. The white insulated boots are the same as the black model, but with an extra layer of insulation. This arctic trooper struggles to light an M1950 mountain stove; on his large ALICE pack is an insulated 1-quart canteen.

D3: Extended Cold Weather Clothing System; 10th Mountain Division (Light Infantry), Ft. Drum, NY

The Army began to issue test models of Gore-Tex®

Enlisted rank insignia—official abbreviation/pay grade follows the rank: *(1)* Private 2—PV2/E2 *(2)*Private First Class—PFC/E3 *(3)* Specialist Four—SP4/E4* *(4)* Corporal—CPL/E4 *(5)* Sergeant—SGT/E5 *(6)* Staff Sergeant—SSG/E6 *(7)* Sergeant First Class or Platoon Sergeant—SFC or PSG/E7 *(8)* Master Sergeant—MSG/E8 *(9)* First Sergeant—1SG/E8 *(10)* Sergeant Major—SGM/E9 *(11)* Command Sergeant Major—CSM/E9 *(12)* Command Sergeant Major of the Army—SMA/E9 (Note: Private 1—PV1/E1 has no insignia. *All higher specialists grades have been eliminated.)

cold weather clothing in the early 1980s, but it was not until 1986 that the ECWCS was adopted for issue to light infantry, Ranger and SF units. Gore-Tex® is a water and windproof laminated membrane fabric which 'breathes', preventing moisture build-up and overheating. The AN/PRC-119 radio began replacing the AN/PRC-77 in 1988; it is a member of the Single Channel Ground and Airborne Radio System (SINCGARS-V) family, which is replacing most current manpacked, vehicle and certain aircraft radios.

D4: Snow Camouflage; 25th Infantry Division (Light), Camp Kami Furano, Japan

Troops training with the Japanese Self-Defense Forces wear a white ski mask-type cap, which can also be used as a helmet cover. The US Navy-issue navy blue watch cap is also authorised. The overwhite parka, trousers and mitten shells are merely a single layer of cotton fabric to provide snow camouflage when worn over the cold-wet and cold-dry uniforms.

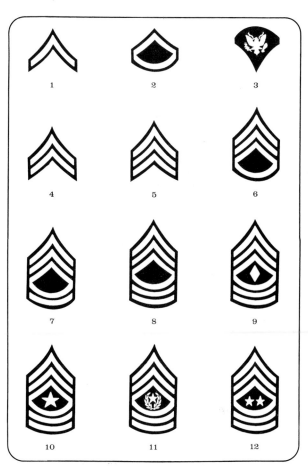

E1: Desert Battle Dress Uniform; 101st Airborne Division (Air Assault), Sharm el Sheikh, Egypt

Battalions of the 82nd and 101st Abn. Divs. and the 197th Inf. Bde. rotate to the Sinai on three month

Officer rank insignia—all are silver except second lieutenant and major, which are gold. Warrant officers' are silver with black squares: *(1)* Warrant Officer 1—WO1/W1 *(2)* Chief Warrant Officer 2—WO2/W2 *(3)* Chief Warrant Officer 3—WO3/W3 *(4)* Chief Warrant Officer 4—WO4/W4 *(5)* Second Lieutenant—2LT/O1 *(6)* First Lieutenant—1LT/O2 *(7)* Captain—CPT/O3 *(8)* Major—MAJ/O4 *(9)* Lieutenant Colonel—LTC/O5 *(10)* Colonel—COL/O6 *(11)* Brigadier General—BG/O7 *(12)* Major General—MG/O8 *(13)* Lieutenant General—LTG/O9 *(14)* General—GEN/O10 *(15)* General of the Army—GOA/O11 (granted only in wartime—the coat of arms is gold with red-white-blue shield).

tours as America's contribution to the United Nations' Multinational Force and Observer (MFO). They wear the MFO patch on their right shoulder and a US flag patch on the left, below their unit patch. All MFO troops wear a 'burnt orange' beret with a small version of the MFO patch. The desert BDUs, introduced in 1982, have a slight drawback in that they were patterned for American deserts and do not sufficiently blend with those of the Middle East. A desert-pattern hat, of the same style as that worn by E2, is also issued. This sergeant operates an AN/PSC-3 satellite communication

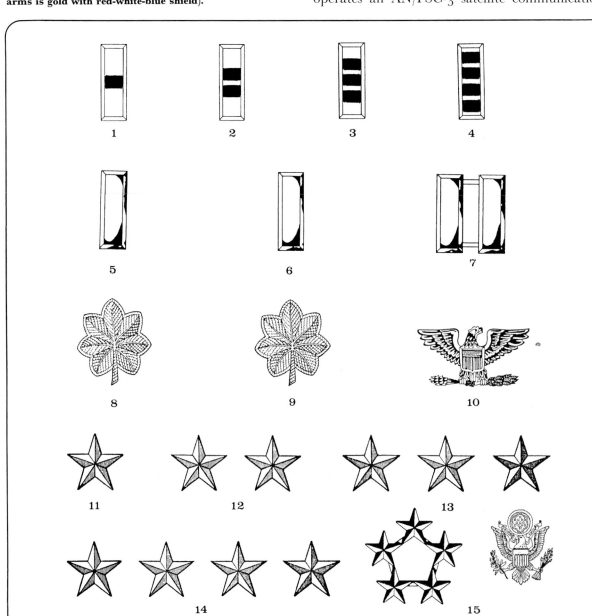

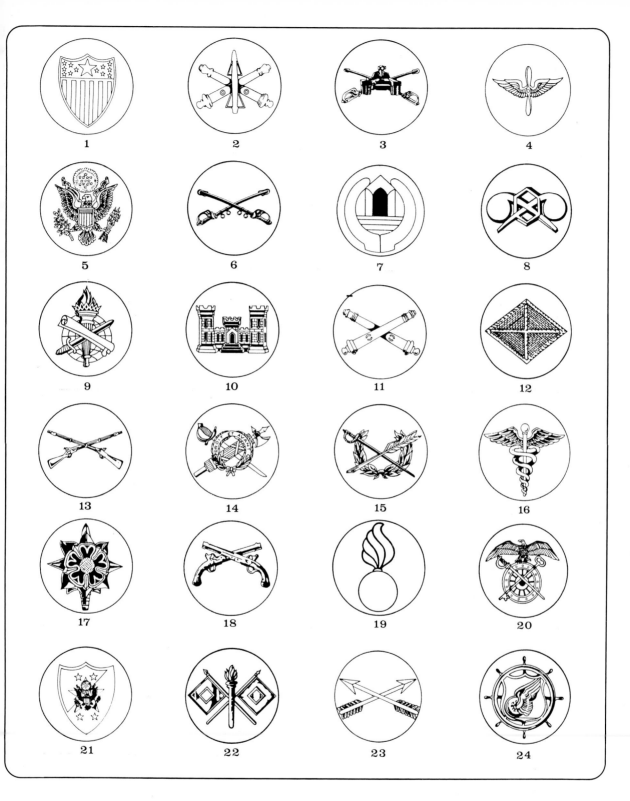

Enlisted branch of service insignia—all are gold: *(1)* **Adjutant General Corps** *(2)* **Air Defense Artillery** *(3)* **Armor** *(4)* **Aviation** *(5)* **Branch Immaterial (for those not assigned to a specific branch)** *(6)* **Cavalry** *(7)* **Chapel Activities Specialist** *(8)* **Chemical Corps** *(9)* **Civil Affairs (RC only)** *(10)* **Corps of Engineers** *(11)* **Field Artillery** *(12)* **Finance Corps** *(13)* **Infantry** *(14)* **Inspector General** *(15)* **Judge Advocate General Corps** *(16)* **Medical Corps** *(17)* **Military Intelligence Corps** *(18)* **Military Police Corps** *(19)* **Ordnance Corps** *(20)* **Quartermaster Corps** *(21)* **Sergeant Major of the Army (red & white shield, counter-charged stars, white centre star, red-white-blue shield)** *(22)* **Signal Corps** *(23)* **Special Forces** *(24)* **Transportation Corps.**

(SATCOM) radio, transmitting a narrow beam to a satellite, which transmits it to a ground station in the US.

E2: Lightweight Battle Dress Uniform; 1169th Engineer Group, Napo Province, Ecuador

ARNG and USAR engineer units rotate to various South and Central American countries for three weeks annual training, to construct roads and take part in other civic action projects. The efforts in Ecuador are particularly gruelling, due to the extremely difficult terrain and climate. This second lieutenant wears the ripstop fabric BDUs, similar to the old tropical uniform (jungle fatigues). These began to be issued in 1986, since the standard BDUs are far too heavy for warm-hot climates. They replaced the OG tropical uniform in 1987, but the tropical combat boots are still issued. Both BDU pattern and OG tropical hats are issued.

E3: Rain Suit; 5th Infantry Division (Mechanized), Ft. Polk, Louisiana

This M60 machine gunner wears the standard rain suit over his BDUs. The green overboots replaced a higher and heavier black model in the early 1980s. Though still wearing an M1 helmet, he has been issued a PASGT helmet cover.

E4: Desert Night Camouflage Uniform; 24th Infantry Division (Mechanized), Egypt

Participating in the bi-annual 'Bright Star' Exercise with the Egyptian Army, this soldier is outfitted with the desert night camouflage parka and trousers, which serve two purposes: providing warmth for cold desert nights (liners are provided), and limiting detection by infrared night vision devices. The suit's grid pattern blends in with an infrared viewer's grid-like screen; its green colour further enhances this effect, as infrared viewer images appear green. He is inspecting an AN/PAS-7 infrared viewer, which uses passive infrared (which cannot be detected like active infrared viewers) to detect thermal signatures of personnel and equipment.

F1: MOPP 4

Mission-Oriented Protective Posture 4 translates to full nuclear, biological, chemical (NBC) protection; MOPP 1 is the field uniform with mask only,

MOPP 2 adds the gloves and hood, and MOPP 3 includes the protective suit. The protective overgarment has a charcoal-impregnated polyurethane foam lining offering six hours of protection from chemical agents. The M17A2 protective mask, coupled with the M6A2 hood, provides excellent defence against NBC contamination. It includes a voicemitter and an integral drinking tube, which when attached to a canteen's M1 NBC cap, permits the wearer to drink. The M17 mask did not have this capability. The M248A1 decon. kit (attached to the mask carrier) is used to decontaminate skin and individual equipment. M9 chemical detection tape is affixed to the suit. He holds an M42 alarm unit, which is attached by wire to an M43 chemical detector placed several hundred metres upwind from a unit's position, allowing early warning of drifting chemical agents.

F2: M25A1 Tank Protective Mask; 11th Armored Cavalry Regiment, West Germany

Armored fighting vehicle crewmen are issued this mask, which utilises a hose and M10A1 filter canister rather than the M17A2's internal filters. It includes an integral microphone permitting hook-up to the vehicle's intercom and radio system. An M5 hood is available, but was deleted here the more clearly to show the mask. The M24 aircraft mask is similar, but can be attached to the aircraft's oxygen supply. The M24 and M25A1 can be worn with the flight and combat vehicle crew helmets.

F3: XM40 Protective Mask

After several unsuccessful attempts to develop a replacement for the M17A2, the XM40 mask was decided upon, though it is not yet being issued.

A & B Officer Branch of Service Insignia—all are basically gold, other colours are identified: *(1)* Adjutant General Corps (silver shield, blue chief, white stars, red & silver stripes) *(2)* Air Defense Artillery *(3)* Armor *(4)* Aviation (silver prop) *(5)* Medical Specialist Corps (black 'S') *(6)* Nurse Corps (black 'N') *(7)* Cavalry *(8)* Chaplain Corps, Christian (silver) *(9)* Chaplain Corps, Jewish (silver) *(10)* Chemical Corps (cobalt blue benzene ring) *(11)* Civil Affairs (RC only) *(12)* Corps of Engineers *(13)* Dental Corps (black 'D') *(14)* Field Artillery *(15)* Finance Corps *(16)* General Staff (silver star, shield as 1) *(17)* Infantry *(18)* Inspector General (blue upper wreath) *(19)* Judge Advocate General Corps *(20)* Medical Corps *(21)* Medical Service Corps (silver, black 'MS') *(22)* Military Intelligence Corps (dark blue petals) *(23)* Military Police Corps *(24)* National Guard Bureau *(25)* Ordnance Corps *(26)* Quartermaster Corps (blue wheel, white edged red hub *(27)* Signal Corps (left flag white with red center, right is reversed) *(28)* Special Forces *(29)* Staff Specialist (RC only) *(30)* Transportation Corps *(31)* Veterinary Corps (black 'V') *(32)* Warrant Officers.

Combat arms branches are identified by their regimental distinctive unit insignia, 'crests'. The various combat support and service support branches are identified by their new corps crests, worn above the left pocket on Class A coats. Most include their branch's colours in their design. The soldier wears the unit's crests to which he is assigned on his shoulder straps and cap. (Sgt. Bert Goulait, *Soldier's Magazine*)

Among its improvements are added comfort, which means longer endurance and increased efficiency while in MOPP 4. The improved chemical protective overgarment features the woodlands camouflage pattern.

F4: Bomb Disposal Clothing System
This suit is intended for Explosive Ordnance Disposal (EOD) personnel, and consists of a fire-resistant Nomex® fabric shell lined with 16 plies of Kevlar® ballistic fabric. Nomex®/Kevlar® spats protect the lower legs and feet. The face shield is made of a polycarbonate/acrylic material mounted on a foam-filled fiberglass chest plate. The effectiveness of the standard PASGT helmet is increased by addition of a bonnet of the same materials and layering as the suit.

G1: CWU-27/P Flyer's Coverall; 6th Cavalry Brigade, Ft. Hood, Texas
This one-piece suit replaced a two-piece model in the late 1970s. The CWU-27/P, like most aviators' clothing, is made of fire resistant Nomex®; both sage green and OG 106 versions are issued. A new

Nomex® BDU-style and pattern suit has begun to be issued. The individual's aviator wings, rank, and name are embossed on a Velcro®-attached leather name tab. The steel-toed flyer's boots use 'D' rings rather than eyelets (to prevent burns caused by metal eyelets) and are lined with glove leather.

G2: MA-1 Intermediate Flyer's Jacket; 1st Armored Division, West Germany
Made of Nomex®, the MA-1 jacket features a reversible international orange lining to aid search and rescue efforts. In garrison officers wear full-colour rank on their caps so they can be more easily identified.

G3: N-2B Cold Weather Flyer's Jacket
The nylon satin N-2B is issued to aviators operating in extremely cold regions. His GS/FRP-2 flyer's gloves are of Nomex® and leather. He carries an individual cold climate survival kit.

G4: SPH-4 Flight Helmet and SRU-21/P Survival Vest
The SPH-4 features a retractable sun visor, boom microphone, and connector permitting all crewmen to enter the aircraft's intercom and radio system. The red and white reflective tape can be applied in several standard patterns; camouflage-pattern tape is also used by some units. The SRU-21/P vest has numerous pockets for a large number of survival items, a survival knife scabbard and revolver holster can also be attached. He holds an AN/PRC-90 radio, used to communicate with search and rescue aircraft.

H1: Tank Commander; 194th Armored Brigade (Separate), Ft. Irwin, California
Participating in a National Training Center rotation, this TC wears the lightweight BDUs. A special Nomex® tanker's suit has been developed, but has not yet been issued. Also under development is a microclimate cooling system ensemble, which cools the individual rather than attempting to cool the entire vehicle interior. The DH132 combat vehicle crew helmet is issued to all crewmen of armored fighting vehicles including commanders and drivers of APCs, IFVs, and SP artillery; it includes a vehicle intercom and radio microphone. The unofficial and privately purchased tanker's boots are without laces and eyelets—the latter can

cause burns in case of a flash fire; a wrap-around leather strap secures the boot. He carries a Korean War era .45 cal. M3A1 submachine gun, still a standard on-vehicle weapon.

H2: Opposing Forces Soldier; 60th Guards Motorized Rifle Division (-), Ft. Irwin, California

This OPFOR soldier of the National Training Center's rôle-playing 'Soviet' unit is actually a member of the 1st Bn. (Mech.), 52nd Inf., 177th Armd. Bde., outfitted in the OPFOR uniform issued through Training Support Centers. It features a 'Soviet' look-alike plastic helmet shell on a US helmet liner, Soviet-style branch of service collar tabs, and slip-on rank shoulder straps, here representing a junior sergeant. Note that OPFOR insignia, while similar to their Soviet equivalents,

are of a different design. He is rigged with XM60 MILES (Multiple Integrated Laser Engagement System) gear, a system of laser detectors which registers 'hits' and near misses from a laser transmitter coded to distinguish the range and killing power of specific weapons, fitted to the rifle or other weapons, including tanks. When 'hit', a buzzer sounds and a light flashes from the alarm carried on his suspenders, and his weapon's transmitter is disabled until turned back on by an umpire. His transmitter will 'fire' when he fires a blank round. Umpires carry hand-held transmitters enabling them to 'kill' selected soldiers, e.g. a leader,

Combat badges—all are silver, infantrymen's badges have a light blue backing: *(1)* Expert Infantryman Badge *(2)* Combat Infantryman Badge *(3)* CIB 2nd award *(4)* CIB 3rd award *(5)* Expert Field Medical Badge *(6)* Combat Medical Badge *(7)* CMB 2nd award *(8)* CMB 3rd award

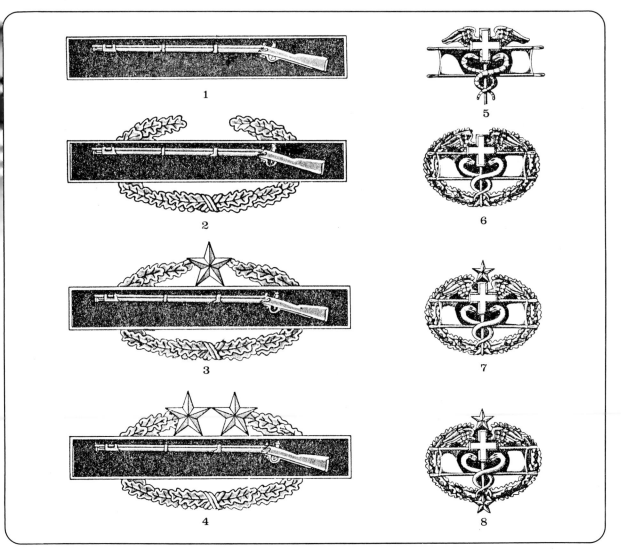

forcing a subordinate to take charge. Extremely realistic, this system also eliminates the old 'You're dead!'—'No I'm not!' arguments.

H3: Mechanic's Coverall; National Training Center Support Battalion, Ft. Irwin, California

This armored vehicle mechanic wears unit-issue OG 106 coveralls and steel-toed safety shoes. 'Class X' BDU's, i.e. worn and stained, are also used by maintenance personnel.

H4: Tank Battalion Commander; 32nd Guards Motorized Rifle Regiment, Ft. Irwin, California

Actually a captain and tank company commander of the 1st Bn., 63rd Armor, 177th Armd. Bde., he plays the rôle of an OPFOR major and tank battalion commander. He wears the OG 507 durable press utility uniform (fatigues), which were no longer authorised after September 1987, but are still used by the '60th Guards Motorized Rifle Division'. A black beret is locally authorised for the unit, and displays his actual rank, the OPFOR star, and OPFOR branch of service insignia. The OPFOR shoulder patch is also worn.

I1, I2: Infantrymen, the immediate future

While much of the gear used by these soldiers is now in the process of being issued, some of it is not yet in wide use. It includes the lightweight BDUs, PASGT vest and helmet, Gargoyles® 'Eye Armor' protective glasses, new combat boots, Individual Integrated Fighting System Tactical Load Bearing Vest, and

Special skill badges—all are silver unless otherwise indicated: (1) Parachutist (2) Senior Parachutist (3) Master Parachutist (4) Second Class Diver (5) Salvage Diver (6) Pathfinder (gold, red & light blue flames) (7) Air Assault (8) Scuba Diver (9) First Class Diver (10) Master Diver (11) Explosive Ordnance Disposal (12) Senior EOD (13) Master EOD (14) Basic Nuclear Reactor Operator (15) Second Class NRO (16) First Class NRO (17) NRO Shift Supervisor (gold).

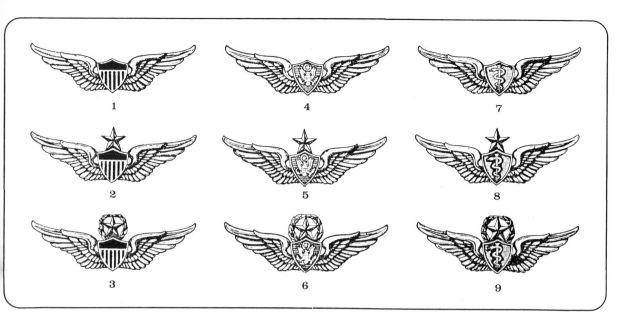

M9 multipurpose bayonet. I1, a light infantryman, is armed with the much improved M16A2 rifle; and carries the new M22 7 × 50 binoculars, which incorporate laser protection filters. I2, a mechanised infantryman, carries an M231 firing-port weapon as used in the Bradley fighting vehicles; outwardly similar to the M16A2, it is internally and functionally different. Bradley infantrymen are also armed with M16A2s for off-vehicle use; he also carries a Swedish-designed 84mm AT4 multipurpose weapon, the replacement for the M72A3 LAW. Fluorescent 'cat's eyes' are displayed on his helmet band, allowing squad members to follow each other at night.

I3: Sniper's 'ghillie suit'; 7th Infantry Division (Light), Ft. Ord, California

The word 'ghillie' comes from the outfits used by Scottish gamekeepers or ghillies, who trained British snipers in the First World War. Snipers make their own suits by gluing protective canvas panels to the shirt and trousers fronts—they crawl a lot. Netting is sewn to the back, and burlap strips and camouflage garnishing are attached. A tropical hat is likewise camouflaged, and a veil added to conceal the face and drape over the rifle. His jungle boots are painted green. He is armed with a 7.62mm M21 sniper rifle, an accurised version of the M14, fitted with a 3-9 × power-adjustable ranging telescope; he carries the new M22 7 × 50 binoculars, incorporating laser protection fitters.

Flyers' badges—all are silver: *(1)* Army Aviator *(2)* Senior Army Aviator *(3)* Master Army Aviator *(4)* Aircraft Crewman *(5)* Senior Aircraft Crewman *(6)* Master Aircraft Crewman *(7)* Flight Surgeon *(8)* Senior Flight Surgeon *(9)* Master Flight Surgeon.

The M21 will be replaced by the Remington 7.62mm M24 bolt-action rifle with a 10 × scope. When crawling, the rifle is protected in a camouflaged 'drag bag'.

J1: Officer's Army Green Uniform; 1st Infantry Division (Mechanized), Ft. Riley, Kansas

The AG 44, 344, or 444 'Greens' are now the standard service uniform since the Army Tan and Khaki uniforms were phased out in 1985. This Class A uniform, i.e. with coat, is worn on and off duty, and while travelling. The Class B version, i.e. without coat, may be worn with either long or short sleeve AG 415 or 428 gray-green shirts; the long sleeve must be worn with a necktie. The enlisted version is similar, but without the black cuff and trousers braid; the service cap is optional for enlisted men. The green shoulder tabs indicate a Combat Leader, here a lieutenant-colonel of the 5th Field Artillery. There is also an optional white version of this uniform.

J2: Enlisted Army Green Uniform; Fourth US Army, Ft. Sheridan, Illinois

This Specialist 4 wears one of many possible combinations of the female AG 344 or 434 classic ensemble, which may be configured with and

1   2   3

4   5   6

7   8   9

10   11   12

without coat, AG 415 or 428 long and short sleeve gray-green shirts, and slacks or skirt. Over the name plate is the crest of the Signal Corps.

J3: Enlisted Pullover Sweater; 7th Transport Group, Ft. Eustis, Virginia

This 11th Trans. Bn. Sergeant 1st Class wears the optional-purchase pullover, modelled after the British 'woolly pully', also worn by females. The same type of shoulder marks are worn on the gray-

Identification Badges—listed in the order of precedence (note: shields on 1 to 5 are red-white-blue): *(1)* **Presidential Service Badge (dark blue backing, gold eagle & edging)** *(2)* **Vice-Presidential Service Badge (white backing, silver eagle & edging)** *(3)* **Secretary of Defense Badge (gold wreath & eagle, silver sunburst)** *(4)* **Joint Chiefs of Staff Badge (silver wreath, gold swords & scrolls)** *(5)* **General Staff Badge (light green leaves, black star, gold eagle)** *(6)* **Guard, Tomb of the Unknown Soldier Badge (silver)** *(7)* **Drill Sergeant Badge (gold, dark green centre backing, black letters & stars)** *(8)* **Military Police Badge (silver)** (Note: recruiter badges are of two ratings awarded in gold and silver.) *(9)* **Army Recruiter Badge** *(10)* **Army National Guard Recruiter Badge** *(11)* **Army Reserve Recruiter Badge** *(12)* **Career Counselor Badge (silver)**.

green shirts; officers' have a thin gold stripe at the base. The AG garrison cap is normal wear for enlisted men. An optional black cardigan (button front) sweater is also authorised.

J4: Officer's Windbreaker
This captain wears another optional item that is seen with gray-green shirts or the pullover sweater. The female beret may also be worn with the classic uniform in lieu of the service cap worn by J2. A black single-breasted raincoat (with zip-out liner), replacing the AG rain- and overcoats, is worn with the Army Green and Blue, and Army White and Blue Mess uniforms.

K1: Enlisted Army Blue Uniform; Guard, Tomb of the Unknown Soldier, Arlington National Cemetery, Virginia
'Blues' are issued only to enlisted personnel whose duties require their wear, as in the case of this guard of the Honor Company, 1st Bn., 3rd Inf. ('The Old Guard'). However, his uniform bears several distinctions that set it apart from the 'normal' Army Blues: authorised wear of sunglasses, Honor Guard tab, Tomb of the Unknown Soldier Guard identification badge, no name plate or rank insignia (for uniformity—NCOs do wear their gold-on-dark-blue stripes), dress belt, and special padded shoes. Only the most select soldiers are chosen for the honor of guarding this shrine, 24 hours a day, 365 days a year.

K2: Officer's Army Blue Uniform
Neither slacks nor or the black beret are authorised with the female 'Blues', worn here by an Ordnance Corps first lieutenant. Male officers wear light blue trousers similar to enlisted men's, including the same width braid. Unit shoulder patches are not worn on 'Blues'.

K3: General Officer's Army Blue Uniform
While the uniform is similar to other officers' 'Blues', general officers wear a different pattern of service cap and dark blue trousers, a distinction dating from the 1840s.

L1: Officer's Army White Mess Uniform
'Mess Whites' are worn at social functions from April until October. Another uniform class based on this is the Army White Evening Mess, worn with a formal dress shirt and white vest and bow tie. For a long time an 'officer's only' uniform, it was authorised for enlisted wear in the mid-1980s, along with the 'Mess Blues': enlisted personnel wear simplified cuff braiding with small gold rank insignia within. Female versions include black and white knee-length and full-length black skirts.

L2: Officer's Army Blue Evening Mess Uniform
This Medical Corps captain, identified by branch of service colour lapel facings, wears the evening mess version of this most formal of uniforms, authorised for year-round wear. The 'Mess Blues' female version uses a knee-length skirt.

L3: General Officer's Army Blue Uniform and Cape
Wearing the generals' version of L1's uniform, this figure demonstrates the principal differences—the sleeve ornamentation and trouser braid. Generals' capes are lined with dark blue while other officers' are lined with their branch colour. Males' capes are knee length and females' finger-tip length.

Notes sur les planches en couleur

A1 Le *battle dress uniform* ou *BDU* est universel. La marque du sergent instructeur est le *Smokey Bear*, inspiré de l'ancien chapeau de campagne M1910. Il porte les écussons d'expert-fantassin et de sergent instructeur. **A2** L'uniforme d'éducation physique, avec tricot de corps et shorts assortis, et chaussures de course, peut être acheté individuellement dans les magasins de l'Intendance. **A3** Pour l'instruction, les soldats portent seulement les casques M1 sans housse ou les casques légers, avec la désignation de la compagnie marquée au pochoir. Le tricot de corps marron a maintenant été remplacé par une version olive. **A4** Avec l'augmentation du nombre des recrues féminines, les sergents instructeurs femmes ont fait leur apparition, avec leur chapeau distinctif.

B *Fireteam* d'infanterie: **B1** chef d'équipe; **B2** grenadier; **B3** artilleur-*SAW*; **B4** voltigeur. Deux équipes constituent une section, commandée par un *staff-sergeant*.

C1 La *2nd Armored Division* porte son insigne '*Hell on Wheels*' sur la poche gauche et non pas sur l'épaule. **C2** Ce *Specialist 4* est équipé du harnachement *ALICE*, introduit en 1974. **C3** Les servants d'artillerie lourde sont armés de pistolets, ici le nouveau *Beretta M9*.

Farbtafeln

A1 Die *Battle Dress Uniform* (Kampfuniform) oder *BDU* ist universell. Kennzeichen des Drill-Sergeanten ist der *Smokey Bear*-Hut, kopiert von dem alten M1910-Hut. Er trägt Abzeichen, die ihn als Infanterie- und Ausbildungsexperten kennzeichnen. **A2** Der Trainingsanzug mit passendem, kurzärmligen Unterhemd, Shorts und Laufschuhen wurden alle private bei der Verkaufsstelle des Quartiermeisters erworben. **A3** Bei der Grundausbildung werden nur unbedeckte M1-Helme oder Helmfutter mit aufgestempelter Kompanienummer getragen. Das braune Unterhemd wurde nun durch ein olivfarbenes ersetzt. **A4** Mit der wachsenden Anzahl weiblicher Rekruten erschienen auch weibliche Drill-Sergeanten mit ihren eigenen typischen Hüten.

B Infanterie 'Fireteam': **B1** Teamführer; **B2** Grenadier; **B3** SAW-Kanonier; **B4** Schütze. Zwei Teams bildeten einen Zug unter Führung eines Staff Sergeant.

C1 Die 2. Armored Division trägt ihr Abzeichen 'Hell on Wheels' auf der linken Brustseite, nicht auf der Schulter. **C2** Dieser 'Specialist 4' trägt die ALICE-Traggurten, eingeführt 1974. **C3** Die Mannschaften für schwere Waffen tragen Pistolen—hier die neue M9 Beretta.

D1 Tenue pour climat froid et humide: sous-vêtements longs, chemise et pantalon de laine vert olive, veste de campagne doublée en toile léopard, pantalon de campagne vert olive—la version de camouflage n'est pas encore disponible de manière générale; et bottes de caoutchouc fourrées. **D2** Tenue pour climat froid et sec—identique à D1, avec l'addition d'une parka et d'un pantalon de caoutchouc, casquette de camouflage fourrée, et bottes fourrées. **D3** La tenue ECWCS est faite de Goretex imperméable. La radio AN/PRC-119 a commencé à remplacer la plupart des autres appareils portatifs en 1988. **D4** Survêtements blancs minces de camouflage, sans valeur protectrice; remarquez aussi la cagoule, utilisable également comme housse de casque.

E1 BDU désertique, avec le béret orange et l'insigne sur l'épaule droite de la Force Internationale des Nations-Unies dans le Sinaï. Ce sergent parachutiste utilise l'appareil de communications par satellite AN/PSC-3. **E2** Version tropicale du BDU, introduite en 1986; on trouve aussi bien des chapeaux olive que des chapeaux de camouflage. **E3** Mitrailleur, portant un combinaison imperméable pardessus son BDU, avec une nouvelle housse de casque 'Fritz' pardessus son vieux casque M1, et des couvre-chaussures verts de 1980. **E4** BDU désertique de nuit, protégeant du froid des nuits désertiques, et permettant d'éviter la détection par instruments à infra-rouges.

F1 Cette appellation fait référence—dans le jargon officiel américain—à la tenue protectrice pour la guerre nucléaire, biologique et chimique, et aux masques M17A2 et M5A2; une trousse de décontamination M248A1 est attachée au sac contenant le masque; il a en mains un dispositif d'alarme M42. **F2** Utilisable avec le casque des équipages de véhicule blindé, ce masque est habituellement associé au masque M5, omis ici pour plus de clarté. **F3** Cet article est à l'essai, et n'est pas encore réglementaire. **F4** Combinaison ignifugée, incorporant le tissu protecteur Kevlar, et masque protecteur en polycarbonate et acrylique.

G1 Vêtement ignifugé, réglementaire depuis la fin des années 70; une nouvelle version de camouflage a commencé à faire son apparition. **G2** Egalement en Nomex, cette veste a une doublure 'orange-sauvetage'. En garnison, tous les insignes sont portés sur la casquette. **G3** Veste de grand froid en nylon satiné, et équipement de survie arctique. **G4** Un équipement complet de survie dans les poches de sa veste, ce pilote communique avec l'avion de secours à l'aide d'une radio AN/PRC-90.

H1 Le BDU léger est porté pour des raisons climatiques; il n'existe pas encore de combinaison légère ignifugée réglementaire pour les équipages de chars. Le casque est le DH132, utilisé par tous les équipages de véhicules blindés. Chacun achète ses brodequins. La vieille mitraillette M3A1 est encore réglementaire à l'intérieur du véhicule. **H2** L' 'ennemi' n'est pas censé être une reconstruction exacte des troupes du bloc soviétique, mais donne simplement une idée du style de leurs uniformes. Le système laser MILES simule les impacts en allumant une lampe et en faisant retentir une sonnerie lorsque l'arme est correctement pointée et tirée à blanc. **H3** Treillis vert olive conventionnel, et brodequins de sécurité à pointes d'acier. **H4** Le treillis OG-507, éliminé progressivement depuis 1987, est encore utilisé par OPFOR (l' 'ennemi'); les galons de capitaine sont portés sur le béret avec les insignes OPFOR.

I1, I2 BDU léger, gilet pare-balles PASGT et casque, lunettes protectrices, nouveaux brodequins de combat, gilet de harnachement IIFSTLBV, fusil M16A2 (I1) et baïonnette M9; l'arme M231 est seulement utilisée dans les hublots de tir du Bradley. Remarquez AT4, arme anti-tank suédoise remplaçant le LAW. **I3** Inspiré des habitudes britanniques, l'équipement du tireur d'élite est fabriqué en cousant toile de jute et autres articles, attachés au filet de camouflage, à la chemise et au pantalon rembourrés du chapeau de brousse. Les tireurs d'élite fabriquent eux-mêmes leur vêtement. Le fusil est le M21.

J1 Les uniformes bronze et kaki ont été éliminés progressivement à partir de 1985; l'Army Green est l'uniforme standard de l'armée, en service commandé ou non. Class A = avec vareuse; Class B = avec chemise gris-vert à manches courtes ou à manches longues, dans ce cas toujours avec cravate. La version pour les autres grades est similaire mais sans revers noir ni soutache de pantalon. Les insignes identifient ici un lieutenant-colonel, du 5th Artillery Field, la bride verte de l'épaulette indiquant un commandant d'une unité de combat. **J2** Une Specialist 4 en uniforme vert; au-dessus de l'écusson portant le nom, l'écusson des Transmissions. **J3** Le calot ('garrison cap') est la coiffure normale pour les grades subalternes. Le chandail, inspiré du style britannique, est facultatif. **J4** Le béret féminin remplace la casquette portée par J2; la vareuse peut être portée avec le chandail ou la chemise.

K1 La tenue bleue de cérémonie n'est réglementaire que pour le personnel en mission spéciale, comme le 1er bataillon, 3ème Infanterie montant la garde au tombeau du Soldat Inconnu. **K2** Version féminine de la tenue bleue, portée par un lieutenant du Service du Matériel. Les insignes de l'unité normalement sur l'épaulette ne sont pas portés sur la tenue bleue. **K3** Une casquette spéciale et un pantalon bleu foncé distinguent la tenue bleue des généraux.

L1 Portée par temps chaud; la tenue de soirée comprend chemise de soirée, gilet blanc et noeud papillon. Cette tenue blanche a cessé d'être exclusivement pour les officiers vers le milieu des années 80; les grades subalternes ont une soutache de revers simplifiée; les femmes portent une jupe noire ou blanche. **L2** Capitaine du Service de Santé en tenue de soirée bleue, avec parements à la couleur du Service. **L3** La tenue des généraux se distingue par la soutache du pantalon et l'ornementation des manches; leur cape est doublée de bleu foncé, celle des autres officiers de la couleur de leur arme.

D1 Uniform für Kälte/Nässe: lange Unterkleidung, olivgünes Wollhemd un Hose, Wald-Tarnjacke und Futter, olivgrüne Hose—Tarn-Äquivalent hier noc nicht allgemein erhältlich; isolierte Gummistiefel. **D2** Kalt/trocken-Uniform wie D1, mit zusätzlicher Kaputze und Arktik-Hose, isolierter Tarnkappe un speziell isolierten Stiefeln. **D3** Die ECWS-Kleidung besteht aus wasserfeste Goretex. Das Funkgerät AN/PRC-119 beginnt seit 1988 die meisten ander tragbaren Geräte zu ersetzen. **D4** Dünne weisse Überwurf-Tarnkleidung oh Wetterschutzeigenschaften; siehe Skimasken-Kappe, auch als Helmüberz verwendbar.

E1 Wüsten-BDU mit orangfarbener Kappe, auf rechter Schulter Abzeichen de UN-Multinationalen Truppe und Beobachtereinheit im Sinaigebiet. Dies Fallschirmjäger-Sergeant benutzt ein AN/PSC-3-Satellitenfunkgerät. **E2** Tro enversion von BDU, seit 1986; es gibt sowohl olivgrüne wie Tarnhüte. **E3** M Schütze mit Regenanzug über seiner BDU, neuem 'Fritz'-Helmschutz über de alten M1-Helm und grünen Überschuhen. **E4** Wüsten-BDU für die Nach schützt gegen kalte Wüstennächte und auch gegen Infrarot-Detektoren.

F1 Diese Bezeichnung bezieht sich in der unverständlichen amerikanische Amtssprache auf den Schutzanzug gegen nukleare, biologische und chemisch Kriegführung, die Maske M17A2 und die Kaputze M5A2; ein Entseuchungssa hängt an seinem Maskensack, und der Alarmgerät M42. **F2** Zu verwende zusammen mit dem Helm von Panzerfahrzeugbesatzungen, ist diese Maske mei kombiniert mit der M5-Kaputze, die hier für klarere Illustration weggelass wurde. **F3** Das ist ein experimentelles Stück, noch nicht allgemein ausgegebe. **F** Feuersichere Overalls mit Kevlar-Schutzstoff und einem Polykarbonat/Akr Gesichtsschirm.

G1 Feuerfester Anzug, ausgegeben zuerst Ende der 70er Jahre; eine neu Tarnversion ist grenade herausgekommen. **G2** Diese ebenfalls aus Nome hergestellte Jacke hat ein orangefarbenes Futter für bessere Sichtbarkeit be Bergung. Im Kasernendienst werden die vollständigen Abzeichen auf der Kapp getragen. **G3** Kaltwetterjacke aus Nylon-Satin; er trägt Arktikausrüstung. **G** Mit umfassender Überlebensausrüstung in den Westentaschen, hält dieser Pilo ein AN/PRC-90-Funkgerät für für Funkverbindung mit einem Bergungsflug zeug.

H1 Leichtgewichtige BDU aus Klimagründen; ein leichtgewichtiger, feuerfest Anzug für Panzermannschaften ist noch nicht herausgebracht worden. D DH132-Helm wird von allen Panzerfahrzeugbesatzungen verwendet. Die Stief sind Privaterwerb. Das alte M3A1-Maschinenpistole wird immer noch zu Tragen im Fahrzeug ausgegeben. **H2** Die 'gegnerischen Streitkräfte' sind nic als exakte Rekonstruktion von Sowjetblock-Truppen gedacht, sondern solle lediglich einen Eindruck von deren Uniformen vermitteln. Das MILES Lasersystem simuliert Treffer durch Aufleuchten einer Lampe und Ertönen Summers, wenn die Waffe richtig gezielt und eine Platzpatrone abgefeuer wurde. **H3** Konventionelle olivfarbene Arbeits-Overalls und Sicherheitsschu mit Stahlspitzen. **H4** Die 1987 abgeschaffte Dienstuniform OG-507 wird imm noch von 'OPFOR' getragen; sein Hauptmanns-Dienstrang wird getrage zusammen mit 'OPFOR'-Abzeichen auf der Kappe.

I1, I2 Leichte BDU, PASGT-Panzerweste und Helm, M16A2-Gewehr (I1) m M9-Bayonett; die von I2 getragene Waffe M231 wird nur in den Schiessschart von Bradley-Fahrzeugen verwendet. Siehe AT4, eine schwedische Pan zerabwehrwaffe als Ersatz der früheren LAW. **I3** Nach britischen Vorbilde besteht diese Heckenschützenkleidung aus Segeltuch- und anderem Ranmateri mit Netzverbindung, aufgenäht auf das schutzgepolsterte Hemd samt Hose un Buschhut. Heckenschützen fertigen ihre eigenen Anzüge an. Siehe M21-Gewe

J1 Braun/khaki-Uniformen wurden 1985 abgeschafft; dieser Anzug in 'Arm Green' ist die Standard-Uniform in und ausser Dienst. Class A = mit Jacke; Cla B = mit lang-oder kurzärmeligem, graugrünem Hemd, stets mit Krawatt Versionen für andere Ränge ähnlich, aber ohne schwarze Manschetten un Hosenaufschläge. Diese Abzeichen kennzeichnen einen Oberstleutnant, 5t Field Artillery, wobei die grüne Schlinge am Schulterriemen den Kom mandanten einer Kampfgruppe kennzeichnet. **J2** Ein weiblicher Specialist 4 i grüner Uniform; über dem Namensschild das Abzeichen des Nachrichtenkorp **J3** Die Feldmütze ist die normale Kopfbedeckung für untere Ränge. Der Pullove wurde als Option gekauft, kopiert nach britischen Vorbildern. **J4** Die Kappe fü Frauen ersetzt das von J2 getragene Käppi; diese Jacke kann als Option mi Pullover oder Hemd getragen werden.

K1 Blaue Galauniform wird nur an Soldaten mit Spezialdienst ausgegeben, wi hier 1.B., 3.Infantry, bei der Grabwache. **K2** Weibliche Version der blaue Uniform, getragen von einem Oberleutnant des Zeugkorps. Regiments Schulterabzeichen werden auf blauen Uniformen nicht getragen. **K** Spezialkappe und dunkelblaue Hose stellen die Generals-Version der blaue Uniform dar.

L1 In warmem Wetter getragen; Die Galaversion hat ein Smokinghemd, weiss Weste und Fliege. Diese weisse Messeuniform ist seit Mitte der 80er Jahre nic mehr nur für Offiziere bestimmt; untere Ränge tragen vereinfachte Manschettenbeschlag; Frauen tragen weisse oder schwarze Röcke. **L2** Hauptmann der Sanitätsabteilung in der Abendversion der blauen Mess euniform, mit Aufschlägen, die seine Abteilung anzeigen. **L3** Hosen- un Ärmelbeschläge kennzeichnen den General; die Umhänge von Generälen sin dunkelblau gefüttert, die anderer Offiziere mit der Farbe ihrer Abteilung.